Living in the Land of Why

Living in the Land of Why

Essays and Stories from the West

Adam Tanous

Aparejo Press

CONTENTS

CONTENTS

For my family—passed and present—who have always been the true source of joy.

And did you get what
you wanted from this life, even so?
I did.
And what did you want?
To call myself beloved, to feel myself
beloved on the earth.

--RAYMOND CARVER, "LATE FRAGMENT"

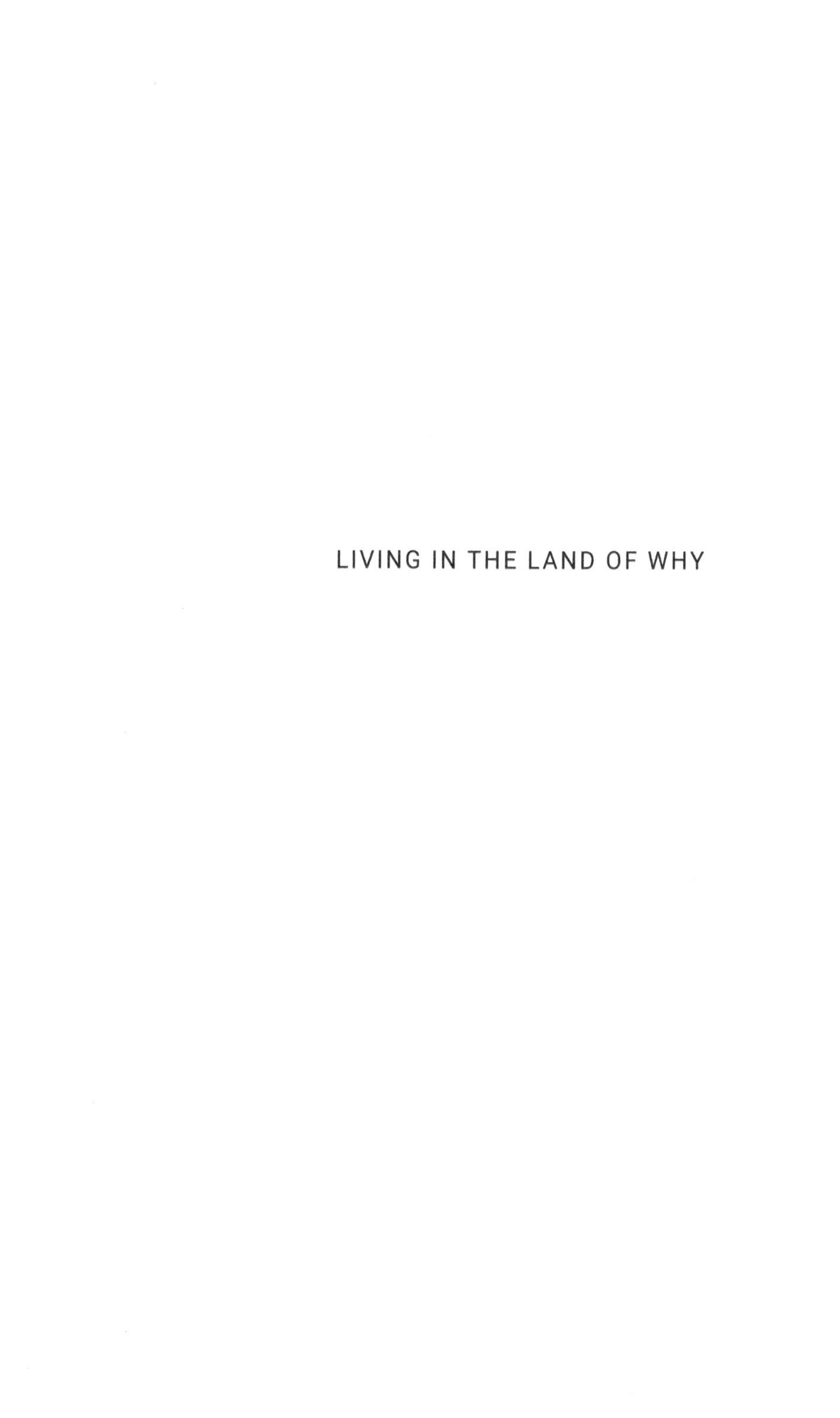

LIVING IN THE LAND OF WHY

Mother's Day, Belated

Time traveling of sorts

A number of years ago, which was likely close to 15, I happened upon a cassette tape. It was there in a cardboard box among several hundred printed photos, device power cords with plug shapes I didn't recognize, and an empty Pee Chee folder. But the cassette caught my eye. Stumbling onto this vestige of technology from a previous century seemed the domestic equivalent of spotting an arrowhead in the brush.

It was a Craig C-60, and so there would be no confusion, the label stipulated what you were getting: "60 Minute Cassette (30 min. per side)." I suppose in an era in which data storage didn't seem infinite as it does now, it wasn't so outlandish to make it clear you weren't getting 60 minutes *per side*.

Also scratched on the label in ball point pen—another gizmo from a previous century first patented in 1888 by John Loud, then improved upon and patented in 1945 by Laszlo Biro—was the word, "MOM," clearly written in MOM's handwriting. The tape was a recorded letter from her sent to me on my birthday in 1980. At the time, she was 47, a nurse, living alone in a tiny African village—Salima, Malawi—working for the Peace Corps and doing whatever she could to improve public health there. Early on, she figured out that the root cause of most health issues there was a lack of clean water. So, much of her time was spent building wells and educating the locals about their value.

I had listened to the letter when I received it in 1980, but not since. It had traveled with me over the years: to college, various apartments and storage units, graduate school, a couple river guide houses, then different real houses as family life evolved. My mom died in 1996, but her cassette carried on its life. Every time I packed up to move, there it was. But when I finally decided that I should listen to it again, tape players were nowhere in sight. Compact discs had taken their place, which had then been made obsolete by MP3 players (iPods), which, in turn, gave way to streaming systems—technology's progenitor cannibalism at work.

With time to kill one day last year, I wandered into a second-hand store in Boise, Idaho. There, for $10, was a GE cassette player. My plan was to play the tape while recording with my computer, thereby preserving her audio letter forever, at least until computers become obsolete. However, reacquainting myself with a cassette player, the first thing I did was break the tape, a Mylar strip barely fifteen-thousandths of an inch thick and an eighth of an inch wide.

After my dad died, which was a few years prior to my mom dying, I remember having an almost Pavlovian response every time I was stumped by something: broken garbage disposal, leaky sprinkler system, tax question, it didn't matter what. I would get up (the days when phones were attached to the wall) to call my dad—he would know. Halfway to the phone, I'd realize he wouldn't be answering. This went on for a year or more. Perhaps a bittersweet fact, but all those dad questions are now answered by Mr. Google, including how to fix a broken cassette tape, which involves a tiny screwdriver, Scotch tape, steady hands, and a good deal of patience. I had two of the four, which eventually proved to be enough. I pushed play on the GE, hit record on my MacBook and left the room. Thirty minutes later, I flipped the tape and went for a run.

Albeit a defunct technology, tape recorders are ingenious little devices. Sounds—nothing more than vibrations in air—are converted into electrical signals that reflect the frequency and amplitude (pitch and volume) of a given sound. The electrical signal is then converted to a magnetic one. When a tape coated with tiny magnetic particles is run by that magnetic signal, the tiny magnets align according to the signal and "store" the pitch and volume at any given moment. To play the sound, the process is reversed. It is nothing short of miraculous and now barely a footnote in the history of technology.

Mother's Day 2021, 41 years after I received the tape, 25 years after my mother had died, and one year after I had finally converted it to a digital file, I listened to MOM, side one and two.

It is startling to hear your mother's voice after not hearing it for all those years. But here she was, on Mother's Day no less, talking to me. Magically, those little magnetic particles had unfurled themselves, come to life in the room, as real as anything around me.

She told me about the little nuances of her day, Sept. 15, 1980; how she and her friend, Mr. Bomberi, had been tanning a goat hide but that something was amiss with the recipe. They had earlier worked on building a mud stove together. She told me that every day when she returned from working in the villages, eight or nine small children greeted her on the dirt road. It was the same exact exchange each day. "Good evening, sir, how are you?" they'd ask my mom in chorus. "I am fine, how are you?" she would say. First one, then all would respond, "I am super!" and then follow her down the road to her house.

She reported that she drank Coke three times a day because when you were out in the villages you could never know about the water. Each Coke was five cents. For a little extra money, you could get a "sandwich," which comprised bread and margarine. Gin, with which she made her nightly Gibson, was $2 for a half-quart. Occasionally, she travelled to Lilongwe to visit other expats for a meal and conversation. And each morning, on a cheap little AM/FM radio, she liked to listen to Voice of America. One particular morning and the only time in two years, she picked up a live broadcast of the San Francisco Giants playing the Philadelphia Phillies. My mom loved the Giants, loved baseball, used to be the scorekeeper for our Little League games, and, of course, was fluent in the curious code of baseball scoring. Telling me about the Phillies game—"a good one" as she said—how could she know that years later my last sweet memory of her would be of her curled up in bed, reeling from cancer, but joyfully listening to the soothing sound of Lon Simmons calling a Giants game?

The recording ebbed toward the 60-minute mark. I started to get nervous as it ticked down, wanting more, wondering how she was going to say goodbye. But she seemed oblivious to the limits of the Craig-C60 and started to tell me another story, this one about making friends with the local witch doctor. Then, oddly, there was another voice on the recording, a child's voice. Was this one of her neighbor children? I played it again; this time I could hear it. It was my youngest daughter, a two-year-old, babbling on with witticisms as she does, seemingly trying to get my mom's attention as she went on about her last visit with the medicine man. For the briefest of moments, I was fooled—they were there, in the same place, same time, same life. My breath held for a beat. Then I knew—my fumbling with two technologies three times-removed had accidentally made the impossible happen. For one shining moment, my mother and daughter—separated by great time and place, even death—were now together.

Then the recording clicked off.

Last Call

Trouble at Troublemaker

I suppose the goats might have been an omen.

But really, who would expect an omen to come along on a Friday afternoon? Right there on the Dwight D. Eisenhower Highway, a bumpy stretch of asphalt choked with commuters and glacier-dooming exhaust?

I was with Buford and Rico—old friends—all of us part-time river guides with much more good humor at our disposal than river skills. Buford was a welder, Canadian Club drinker, and a man with a merciless wit. Rico I've known for the great majority of my life, and I can say that during most of that time together we were laughing about one thing or another.

We were on I-80, somewhere between San Francisco and Placerville. People with real jobs were jockeying around for the exits of an endless string of suburban gems—San Pablo, Pinole, Hercules, Living Hell. We, on the other hand, were on our way to kayak and otherwise fritter away another weekend of our precious lives on the South Fork of the American River.

Buford was driving, clipping along at 70. I can't say why except to chalk it up to the screwy power of omens, but the three of us glanced over at the car next to us at the same moment. Just spitting distance away was a Ford Country Squire station wagon. It was an old car, sun-bleached and rusty in places. A beaten down, 60-year-old white guy was driving. I was transfixed by him, and yet wholly unable to form the thought of what I was seeing. Rico, even more voluble than I, seemed equally perplexed. Finally, Buford, ever the man to unveil an elephant in the room, proclaimed, "Goddamn, that car is chock full of goats."

Indeed, there were 20—maybe more—live goats stuffed in the back of the Country Squire station wagon, all standing stem to stern, packed like so many sardines in a can. Equally unnerving, the fellow driving seemed absolutely nonplussed by it all. He was idly staring off into the middle distance, as if he were pondering whether he had left his stove on at home.

A carload of goats? Theories came to mind: a relationship gone sour? Had this poor bastard finally mustered the courage to leave a soul-crushing marriage, just packed up his goats and left? Or—it was a stretch—but could he be involved in some sort of bizarre animal trafficking? These did not look like particularly rare goats—something, say, worthy of trafficking. But, then again, could I pick a black-market tortoise from of a lineup of house turtles? Probably not.

And then the basic logistical questions came to mind. How did he get them in the car in the first place? What could the inside of that Country Squire possibly smell like? Did he have food in there for them? Having suffered a summer at an Idaho river guide house with a goat named Achmed, I know a thing or two about goats. One is that they eat incessantly, and it doesn't seem to matter if it is of this Earth or not. I suppose it was possible that this guy pulled over at rest stops and let them graze a bit. But, really, how did he manage that? And where in God's name was he going with a carload of goats? It was all so puzzling.

It was puzzling but great fodder for the rest of the drive. That was all it took with the three of us: one weird little moment and we could launch into hours of bantering back and forth, each of us trying to out-funny the other guy. And this, it has occurred to me over time, is really the heart of river guiding. In fact, it is the enduring memory of my working on rivers for much of my adult life—not the whitewater, not the stillness of river canyons, nor the space-blue skies under which I have been sheltered for so many days. Rather, it is simply the relentless pursuit of laughter. It might start with someone finding a decrepit bone in camp, say, a raccoon or a marmot jawbone—nothing regal, certainly. And though they may be otherwise intelligent people, river guides will spend hours trying to make each other laugh with that stupid little bone. The effort is unremitting and exhausting, but as much fun as anything I've ever done.

By the time we reached the guide house, we had played out every imaginable goat scenario. The air had finally cooled, and we settled in for dinner with a couple of other guides. The house, which was as close to a commune as you might experience during the Reagan era, did, in fact, have a spectacular perch over the South Fork of the American River. It also had a scratchy green carpet, furniture a smart man would never sit in, and dust —all the dust of Ethiopia in one little house. By the time we had had our fill of cheese quesadillas and leftover beer it was 11 p.m.

"How about a quick pop at the Round Tent?" Buford said in his usual peppy way. "Last call and all."

The Round Tent was a bar in Placerville and not one at which river guides were particularly welcome. Hard, tough men living with a bit of a bitter taste in their mouths drank there. We were the antithesis of all that: soft and weak, full of laughs and bright futures. Still, we knew our way around a bar.

Chris, a young and strapping guide, eager to be a part of the fun, chimed in, "Is it alright if I come?"

We all considered the moment, though perhaps a little longer than we should have. Again, it was Buford who broke the silence.

"Chris, I like to drink," he said sternly. "So does he, and so does he. And when we drink together, we really like to drink."

"Oh, I'm in," Chris said. "I AM IN."

Of course, last call wasn't technically last call. There were shots that went around—Canadian Club, tequila, ouzo. There were beer chasers and Kahlua nightcaps. And miraculously, as if the hand of God had reached down and touched us, there we were in the Round Tent Bar in Placerville, California, the four smartest and funniest guys in the whole wide world. Certainly, we needed a bigger stage.

Along the winding road to South Lake Tahoe, Nevada, Chris discovered some ugly truths about the life of a river guide.

After he threw up the first time, we pulled over and cleverly put him in the back of the pickup. There was a camper shell and plenty of fresh air, but that was about it. And for fear he might be a sleepwalking drunk, we locked the camper shell. That was that; our woes were literally behind us. We carried on, as if we were people with something vitally important to do.

Caesars Tahoe at 2 a.m. was everything we had hoped—loud, fun, full of crowded craps tables and pretty women to flirt with. Even the pit bosses seemed cheerful. We were winning money but not enough to alarm anyone. Nobody in the casino was having more fun than we were. Bernadette, a tall and pretty black woman, was quick to notice and sidled up to us.

She said she was the headline comedienne at the casino, though it occurred to me she wasn't all that funny. Nonetheless, she seemed to think we were amusing, so that was something. My suspicion and deep fear was that she might be a hooker with a nasty pimp and that, somehow, this was how the fun would end. We'd wake up on some dirt road outside of town, toothless and broke.

But lovely Bernadette proved me wrong. She simply thought it might be fun to throw in with some mildly entertaining fools for a bit. And who were we to refuse the company of a beautiful woman with access to all the comps a casino had to offer?

After several rounds at the craps table, Bernadette invited us to a party in her suite. Granted it wasn't Las Vegas, but it was quite nice—spacious, big hot tub in the living room, views of the Tahoe strip.

As the night wore on, all sorts of people rolled in and out of the suite. Presumably, they were Bernadette's friends, but who knows who they were? There was plenty of champagne, dancing, soaking in the hot tub. Room service appeared more than once. We ate eggs and bacon, French toast, lox. Someone ordered a roast chicken.

When I woke up, I was heartened to discover that I was not face down in some meth head's crappy little yard. All 32 teeth were in place, and, as far as I could tell, I hadn't been robbed. I was, in fact, still in Bernadette's suite, folded into an over-stuffed leather chair.

In the floor-to-ceiling windows, a giant orange sun was rising over the Sierras and the middling high-rises of South Lake Tahoe. It was beautiful and not a bad way to wake up after an all-night party. Rico was across the room sleeping in an odd little Roman couch. Buford was in the king bed, snoring like only a welder can snore. Bernadette and friends were nowhere to be seen.

At that moment, I remembered Chris in the Caesars parking lot. Locking the camper shell seemed brilliant at the time. Now, I wasn't so sure.

"Shit, we've got to go," I announced to nobody in particular.

Happily, we had only our wits to gather—no bags to pack, no bills to pay. Four minutes later we were marching across the parking lot. The Caesars marquee towered above us, Bernadette's name spelled out in little round light bulbs.

All of us were a little nervous as to what we would or wouldn't find in the truck. Buford unlocked the camper shell. Mercifully, Chris had not choked to death on his own vomit. He was sleeping like a teenager on the metal truck bed. He didn't seem to know or care what he had missed. He did seem concerned that he was due to lead a commercial river trip in a few hours and here he was with us in a casino parking lot, a river nowhere in sight.

As much as Rico, Buford, and I wanted to while away the day playing Keno in South Lake Tahoe, our consciences got the better of us. Chris had a trip to run; we had to get him there. Albeit grudgingly, we filled the truck with gas and hustled back down Highway 50 to Placerville. We dropped Chris at the river put-in with a hearty handshake and a tall cup of coffee.

Two hours later, after our second breakfast of the morning, Rico and I were on the river. Kayaking was the perfect hangover recipe: refreshing and quiet. Our day moved along swimmingly—that was until we approached Troublemaker: a class III, sometimes class IV rapid. I had an inkling things weren't quite right when I started to see people clamoring about on both sides of the river. We paddled into the eddy above Troublemaker. I could hear country music playing out of boom boxes.

Clusters of people were gathered around the rapid. Some were in lawn chairs drinking beer, others climbing over boulders. Toddlers were on the shoulders of their dads. It might have been a lovely summer barbecue except for one thing: the ropes. Ropes were stretched across the river from both sides, all connecting at the Troublemaker rock, the heart of the rapid. There, plastered to the rock with the full force of the river, was not one boat but two boats. It was the perfect double wrap.

My heart sank. There, scrambling from one side of the rock to the other, sweat spilling off his brow, was Chris. He looked spindlier than before, and there was a desperate look in his eyes.

It was the look of a man willing to do just about anything to change the trajectory of his life.

Over the noise of the rapid, men were shouting unintelligible and, no doubt, unhelpful instructions to him. Dusty little kids were chucking sticks into the river; dogs were fetching them. And the Placerville heat, dry and crushing, seemed only to magnify the confusion. It was awful—the river guide equivalent of being stoned to death in the town square.

Rico and I were still in our kayaks, bumping around in the eddy, as yet unnoticed by the crowd. Rico turned to me, "Dear God. The poor bastard. We should do something."

"Oh, I think we've done enough," I said.

And with that, we slipped out of the eddy. Heads shamefully bowed, two snakes in the water, we paddled out into the rapid, past Chris and the ugly snarl of gear, ropes, and humiliation.

Though I never saw him again, I know Chris got off that rock. I'm sure he went on to become a fine man, to meet better people and have a better life. It wouldn't have taken much.

Rico and I paddled down river another mile or so and had lunch beside the river. There was a big oak there, so we lay down under it to nap for a bit. I fell into a half-sleep, and my mind drifted back to the goats. I wondered how they had fared. I suspected that they would reach their destination safely. It might take days, but the Squire—dependable, if weary—would deliver them. No doubt it would be a brilliant morning when they arrived, the sun spilling over the hills. Someone young and clear-eyed would see the car roll to a stop, then sprint across a great field, fling open the tailgate. In a burst of hope, a carload of goats would bolt for freedom, each and every one leaping for a life in some verdant land far away.

Finding America at the Little Britches Rodeo

What does it mean to feel patriotic?

There was a time when I spent long summers in Salmon, Idaho, guiding on the Middle Fork and Main Salmon rivers. As guides, we weren't actually in Salmon very much. With 6-day trips and a launch every 8 days, we found ourselves in town for about 24 hours each week, enough time to do laundry, shower, pick up mail, call home, repair cracked hands and feet, eat a meal you didn't cook, and, occasionally, go for a night out.

One such night, we went to the Little Britches Rodeo, which was held at the county fairgrounds just north of town. It was a warm evening, the air sweetly pungent with the smells of tilled soil, sweet alfalfa, and a Noah's Ark of animals roaming the farms nearby. In a place like this, everything on the land, in the air, is alive. And being on the 45th parallel—which you cross just before driving into Salmon from the south—means it's balmy and light long into what you think should be nighttime.

Promptly at 8 p.m., a deep baritone voice came over the P.A. system. We stood: four river guides in shorts and flip flops and a couple hundred more spectators in Wranglers, shirts with pearly snaps, and stiff, cream-colored cowboy hats. Hats went to hearts. Ten little girls on full grown horses ambled into the arena, then trotted around its edge, each bearing an American flag, their hair streaming behind them. The national anthem began, and we all sang. Even the children in the stands, some not more than five or six years old, knew the words. They sang with eyes shining. The Bitterroot Mountains loomed above the fairgrounds, stunning and forthright. Mesmerized by the heavy cadence of hooves in the soft dirt, seeing the strength and conviction in the eyes of those little girls, I became lost in the stars and stripes spinning before me. Something welled up and overcame me.

Many days I've wondered why; what swept me up that evening? What was it about that scene that made it seem like America—the idea, the people, the country—was coursing through me? And what exactly does it mean to feel patriotic?

Often patriotism is identified with war, the military, and those who have fallen in war. "The Star-Spangled Banner" itself, originally a poem by Francis Scott Key, describes a battle during the War of 1812, one in which our flag—15 stars and 15 stripes at the time—survived the assault of the British in a Baltimore harbor. In opposition to a foe comes unity and with it a commonly experienced form of patriotism.

But I was part of a generation—the tail of the baby boomers—that slipped into the rare gaps in our history of wars. We were too young for the big ones—WW I and II, Korea, and Vietnam—and too old for the conflicts in the Mideast: The Gulf War, the War in Afghanistan, and second Iraq War. Military life was barely on our radar of consciousness. I've since become acutely aware of its power.

A number of times over the years, I guided a group of guys down the Middle Fork who served together in Vietnam. The intensity of their bond, their devotion to those who hadn't survived is remarkable. They had been together in the war for a year or two, maybe three. Still, here they were decades later holding each other up, toasting friends and experiences we cannot know. I've always admired the depth of their relationship.

So, I can follow a thread of patriotism that weaves through war, friendship, and death. And it may be that it is death that most ties us together. Working as a ski patrolman for many years, I and other patrolmen have been in situations in which, despite our efforts, someone leaves the world before our eyes. The sanctity of the moment joins the survivors in a bond that resists the wear of time and distance.

Driving into the fairgrounds parking lot that night it hadn't really dawned on me what "Little Britches" actually meant. Of course, it referred to children. These were children, 5 to 18 years old, riding animals that didn't seem at all proportionally small or tame. I couldn't believe what I was seeing. The broncos bucked furiously, pounded the earth with hooves, arched their bodies skyward. Boys were hanging on seemingly unafraid, bouncing above the broncos. Ultimately, they all fell, slapped the soft dirt like rag dolls, not far, it seemed, from the wild action of the horses' hooves. Rodeo clowns moved in quickly, but it was harrowing to watch.

Then came a kid named Skeeter from Billings, Montana, who couldn't have been older than 11 or 12. Skeeter mounted his bronco in the loading pens across the way. Several men helped. When the iron gates opened, Skeeter's horse broke out. The other broncos had exploded upwards trying to throw their riders. Skeeter's horse charged forward. It bolted straight across the arena towards the grandstands. At the wooden railing not more than 20 feet away from us, the bronco started to pull up. Surely, I thought, the fence will be indestructible. But the loud splintering of wood shattered that illusion. The horse cracked through the fence, bucking forward and over, following its own front hooves. Skeeter sailed. People stood, screamed. The bronco was now 10 feet away, on its back, rolling from side to side trying to find its footing. Then, in an instant, the horse was up and broke forward in a sprint along the outside of the ring and out of sight.

With the horse gone, we all stood there stunned, staring at Skeeter limp in the dark soil. There was no sound, no motion in the stands. Rodeo workers raced to the boy's side. Time seemed to stretch out forever, dread sinking into the collective psyche. Then little Skeeter stirred, moved a bit more, rolled to his back, and sat up. When that boy walked off, everyone in the place was standing, clapping, crying. For the second time in one night, I felt part of something bigger.

All these years later, the event seems clearer to me. Yes, patriotism can be borne of anger and aggression—unity in opposition to someone or thing or entity. But it can also be forged among disparate lives and lifestyles and beliefs with a common connection. Just as bonds can form in death and in opposition to the other, it, too, can form in aspiration, in bright life moving forward.

IV

The Lives We Never Know

As we go, so go others

There is an old photograph that hangs in the stairway of my house. The photo is taken from above, looking down at my dad and two medical school buddies crowded on to a lounge chair beside a pool. They are at a party. Their faces are bright with laughter; the California sun splashes over them. Youth, joy, friendship, promise—it is all there in black and white.

While the photo captures the joy of that moment, it also haunts me a bit. What haunts me is what's not there: the narrative, the texture and depth of those lives. Looking at the boyish image of my dad from the perspective of the camera peering down, I think of accounts one reads about people who have "died" on the operating table but then have come back to life. In these after-life experiences people describe being above the action, separate from the world but eyeing it as it happens. I get the same feeling from this photo, except it is I who is above the action—not alive but not dead—at least yet. It's a glimpse of a father's life before he was my father.

When we think about our parents, it always has a restricted frame: from some point early in our lives until they pass. But what about their lives before us?

I often think about my life before kids—all the adventures, friends, relationships, work triumphs, disappointments, decision points, great fun and laughter—memories so dear to me but so much of it inaccessible to my children. Surely, my dad had a life that was as vibrant and rich—just different stories, people and places. I hope so, but I will never know for sure.

Sometime after college—I was probably 25, my dad 56 or so—the two of us were driving back from duck hunting near Los Banos, a small town in California. I was driving; he was in the passenger seat watching the grassy hills of the Pacheco Pass roll by. He made an offhand comment about dying: that when he died, so too would die his memories of his family (my dad was the youngest of 11). With his passing, the lives of his siblings would fade with him.

Later in the drive, he fell asleep, his hands folded in his lap. Though he was as healthy as could be at the time, glancing over at his hands, I had a brief vision—as if my psyche were daring itself to inch up to a cliff—of what it would be like when he died. His hands would be folded like this. And for the briefest of moments, I was completely unmoored from the world.

Six years later, in the final days of his life, I was visiting with him at his home. He was in bed, dying of cancer. There was a skylight above us, which he eyed as we talked. Our conversation was halting; both of us knew the trajectory of things.

"That's where I'd like to be," he said suddenly, staring above.

I looked up, through the skylight. There, high above the house, was an eagle sailing in a perfect blue sky. Never in all the years I had known him—32 at that point—had he revealed even a hint of want or need. He was a doctor, always deflecting attention to others and their needs. That's when the full weight of hurt came tumbling down.

'm not an even remotely superstitious person, but now eagles seem like visitations from another world. I doubt it, but just maybe he can see all that has happened since he left. At least, to quote the end of a good and famous story: "Isn't it pretty to think so?"

Would our lives be as precious if they didn't end? I wonder if it is simply their finiteness that crystalizes into memory the joy we find, allows us to hold it to the light, and, if we're lucky, catch the sun for a moment or two.

It pains me to write this, but when I die all the memories of my dad and his siblings will perish, too. In a sense, we all die twice: once when we physically leave the world, and a second time when those a generation below us pass.

Writers, generally, spend their days trying to defy this reality. It is part of our work—some say affliction—to put our lives out into the ether, to document events, thoughts, emotions, memories. And there is a chance—not a big one, but a chance—some of it will be preserved, maybe passed along. If we are lucky, those memories might live on another generation or two. Will the true depth of feeling, the texture of that life reveal itself? Probably not how we hope. But somebody down the way just might be inspired by something someone did or said in a world they can barely imagine.

Sadly, most people, including my father, don't record the nuances of their lives. And so, I am left with a photograph of him laughing with friends, in the prime of life, basking in a sunny future. What are they laughing about? Who are his friends, and what have they gone through together? What brought them to that sunny day beside a pool? What was to happen to my dad's life in the moments and days and years after that photo was taken but before I appeared?

The questions just hang in the air.

We know our family as we know no one else. Still, there is a certain tapestry of their lives that we will never get to touch. I desperately long to know it, but, in the end, it is theirs. And, I suppose, it is theirs to take with them.

V

Give 'em Their Head

Trust is a tricky thing

've never been much of a horseman, though horses and I have crossed paths many times over the years. One of my earliest memories of being on a horse would probably qualify as scarring.

I was 10, living in Africa with my parents, a doctor and a nurse who had decided at ages 41 and 37 to move their young family to Kenya for a while. That wasn't the scarring part. For my brother and me, Kenya was the ultimate playground—a whole country full of dangerous animals, camping in the wild, and soccer (football, we learned), played barefoot and with a tennis ball.

The part I didn't like about living in Africa was that often on Sundays we packed into our old Land Cruiser and drove the Ngong Road from Nairobi to the town of Karen and the home of the Cunninghams.

The Cunninghams were missionaries and perfectly nice people who regularly hosted big picnics for all the ex-pats in the area. Kenya was an independent country at the time, but just barely. The atmosphere was still markedly colonial; the British were everywhere. The rub with the picnics was that before or after each one, I had a riding lesson nearby in Karen. Why I was doing this I have no idea. I had no interest in horses, and my parents certainly were not horse people, didn't even ride.

As it happened, my riding teacher was British—very British and stern and old and a colonel in Her Majesty's Armed Forces. He followed me around the arena on his horse, riding crop in hand. When my horse or I balked at the barrel, or little wooden gate we were supposed to sail over, the Colonel let the crop fly on my horse's haunches. You wouldn't think a 1,200-pound horse with a 90-pound boy on it could accelerate very quickly, but you'd be wrong. It was a little taste of terror every Sunday. I still think about that jackass (the Colonel, not the horse) every time I ride.

I felt a similar surge of terror the first time I crossed a river on a horse. Happily, I was an adult and with a friend who knew quite a bit more about horses than I did. As we rode down the rocky bank to the river—a good 75 yards of flowing river to cross —he said, "Give 'em their head."

Hmmmmm.

As I manhandled the horse right and left to where I thought we should cross, it became obvious to everyone, including my horse, that I didn't know what the hell I was doing, nor what my friend was talking about.

"Let up on the reins," he said. "Give him his head. He'll know where to go."

Halfway across the river, water at my boots, I started to relax. My horse, despite his rider, actually did know what he was doing. I had spent years studying science, worked as a scientist with very smart people. And yet, somehow the concept of evolution hadn't occurred to me: that horses had been crossing rivers for eons, long before anyone decided to get on their backs to do it. To state the obvious: Grass isn't always on your side of the river.

Ironically, it took a horse (and a long-dead British colonel) to crystallize in my mind the Herculean struggle all parents grapple with: trust. Most parents will say they trust their kids. Sure, trust them to do their homework, mow the lawn, turn in their liability release for field trips. But what about when there are real consequences? Like finding yourself underwater with 1,200 pounds of horse on top of you.

Parents reach that moment of giving 'em their head at different times in life; some never do. I remember one summer crossing southern Wyoming with my son and oldest daughter. We were on I-80, which, for the uninitiated, is about as close to the Wild West as you will ever experience. The speed limit is 80 mph, which means everyone drives 90 to 100 mph, some faster. There are streams of semi-trucks, and not just 18-wheelers, but triple rigs, which are basically little trains without the tracks to contain them. Then there is the wind. My god, the wind. It is incessant and, given time, will make a man insane.

My son had his driving learner's permit and, of course, wanted to drive everywhere, every day. (In Idaho, where I live, kids can get driving permits at a ridiculously early age, sometimes 14). So, suddenly, there I was in the passenger seat—young daughter in back—rocketing across Wyoming certain we were destined for a fiery crash.

Hours later, terror transmuted to confidence, which, in turn, burnished into trust. It takes a while and is wholly uncomfortable, but sometimes you just have to get across the river.

One last horse story. My dad, who is no longer alive, always had a distinct red mark on his forehead. Throughout childhood, I was sort of fascinated by it. Apparently, he had been kicked by a horse when he was young. When I was about 20 or so, somehow that mark came up, and I asked my dad how it actually happened; how was he not killed by the kick?

His smile broke slowly, then blossomed. There was no horse, no life-altering blow to the forehead. It was just a run-of-the-mill birthmark and a long-running joke between my parents.

Of course, there were more revelations. Soon thereafter, I also learned that, in fact, my mom had not really dated the tallest man in the world, Henry Hite (8' 2"), after all.

Turns out, trust is more complicated than it seems.

VI

The Scout

When the water comes up

Every river guide has a high-water story. If they don't, they should make one up early on because at some point in their careers they are going to need one. The conversation around a river campfire inevitably turns to them.

Someone will casually throw one out into the general banter. The story often starts with a tired cliché along the lines of: "No shit, there I was," which is just a subtle way of saying, "Am I not just the most bitchin' person you know?" Once the gauntlet has been thrown down, it's then a matter of each guy topping the guy or gal before him.

Silly as it may sound, having a high-water story then telling a high-water story is a ritual of being a river guide. However tiresome, it's just part of the culture. It reminds me of something the now deceased author James Salter said at a lunch with a bunch of us in graduate school. My friend, Lolis, asked him, "Are you in to Jazz?" With a hint of resignation Salter said, "Well, sure. You have to be, I suppose. They're always dragging you to those places."

A curious trait of high-water stories is they change over time. The water gets higher, the heroics more heroic, and, of course, the teller of the tale invariably comes out looking good. And like fish stories, the numbers are always bigger than they could possibly be. *I'm not kidding; he was underwater for 17 minutes. And then I saved his life.* Of course, this begs the question: What were you doing for the first 16 minutes?

Despite how cool and dramatic the stories may seem in the telling, the reality of high-water trips is that they are really only fun after they are over. During the trip, everyone is uptight and nervous, worried about making a mistake and ruining the trip for everyone else. It's less of a happy summer experience and more like waiting to get your teeth drilled.

The real rub of high-water trips is that they invariably involve scouting a rapid or two, which, in my mind, is like getting a prostate exam *while* having your teeth drilled. In other words, I desperately hate scouting rapids, though I admit it is sometimes a necessary evil.

For those unfamiliar with rivers, scouting is pretty much what you would think: getting a good look at a rapid from the shore before you actually run it.

The scout, particularly in a high-water situation, usually begins hundreds of yards upstream of the rapid of concern. This is because the water is moving so fast and the eddies are so few and far between that you want to make sure you can get pulled over in time. Once you spot an impossibly small eddy amid the

11-mile-per-hour current, the trick is to get to it and stay in it. So, you end up coming in at 11 miles per hour, slamming into the rocks on shore, and, in one awkward motion, shipping your oars, scrambling over your paying guests and gear, grabbing the bow line, jumping onto wet, sharp rocks, and holding those 1,500 pounds in place long enough to tie it off. If all goes well, you have not slipped and smacked your knee on a metal box or clocked a guest with an errant oar. Trust me, the Three Stooges could not choreograph this sequence.

With the boat safely tied off, it's time to calmly explain to your guests why exactly you are leaving them in a boat tied to a rock, the river surging, in the middle of the wilderness, to have a look at a rapid you've run a hundred times.

Well—your guests are thinking—*why in the world does he have to **look** at the rapid? Has he not done this before? My god, honey, our children are on this boat. Who is this clown?*

The guides then head down a trail, or over more sharp rocks if there is no trail, in what often feels like a Bataan Death March, until finally reaching a vantage point over the rapid. And there you are with four other guides staring at a rapid that looks much scarier than you imagined. As adrenaline eats through your stomach lining, you very casually talk over the crux of the problem before you.

The first question to answer is: Where is the current flowing? Usually, you want to go where most of the river is going. The second issue at hand is to figure out where the big "holes" or obstacles are. A hole is a section of river where the current flows over a big rock below the surface. As the water goes over the rock it curls back on itself, creating a chunk of river that recirculates.

Third, you want to figure out where you want to end up, that is, beyond staying alive long enough to tell a high-water story. In fact, sometimes a scout takes place in reverse; you find the endpoint you like and visualize a path back upstream to the approach.

Once the problems are identified, the discussion turns to the possible lines to take, how to line up for the right line, and so on. It's agonizing because you're nervous, verging on nauseous, and some guides try to quell that nervousness by incessantly talking about the problem—talking through every imaginable scenario or stroke he or she is going to take. It goes on and on and on, until finally I or someone else equally impatient will snap and say a little too harshly, "We have to go before I throw up on you."

On the way back to the boats, I have a habit—some call it a tic—of stopping every 20 or 30 yards to look at the river, trying to memorize marker points—weirdly shaped trees, or rocks—so I know exactly where I am at any given time during the approach. It almost never works.

Back at the boat, the guide once again has to put on a good show—cool as can be—for the guests. "Looks good. We'll be just fine," you say. If they knew how shaken you really were by what you've seen, they'd never leave that shore.

Pulling back into the current after a scout always feels pretty good. The doing takes the edge off the anticipation of the doing. The oars feel right in your hands, you get a sense of the water again. You know how to row a boat, if nothing else.

But then you get to the entrance to the rapid and suddenly your memory begins to get fuzzy. It's as if you're having a mild stroke—*Shit, was I supposed to be just right or just left of that little rock? Is that the pyramid rock Danny was talking about, or just another goddamn rock? Wait a minute, am I even in the right channel? Goddamnit, why is Del so far ahead of me? I can't' see where he's going.* Then before you know it, you're wondering whether you left the stove on back at the guide house.

One of the first times I ever scouted a rapid was on the Tuolumne River in California. I was training to be a guide there with several other young guides. Danny Bolster, one of the most accomplished boatmen I've ever known, was our trainer. And he had what I think was a photographic memory when it came to scouting rapids. I didn't know this until later when I worked with him, but he could look at a rapid for 20 seconds, then on the walk back to the boats describe every hole and rock, where the eddies were, which currents he would catch—it was uncanny. I would just nod knowingly, pretending that I knew what the hell he was talking about. My default position quickly developed into: *I'll just follow Danny.*

For our first training trip, the river was running at 6,000 cubic feet per second, which, for that river qualifies as high water. We scouted a rapid called Gray's Grindstone. Looking from shore, it was impossible to miss the ledge hole—about the size of a Ford F-150—at the top of the rapid. Below that was a thousand yards or so of holes and standing waves, but nothing as daunting as the entrance hole. We all talked about the line to take. Basically, we would enter backwards—because a rower has more strength pulling than pushing the boat—at an angle to the left and skirt the monster reversal. After that, it would be just "read and run."

So, I thought I knew where the Gray's Grindstone hole was, but it soon became clear that I didn't because I hit the gut of it, which amounted to hitting a 20-foot wall of water. My 16-foot raft surfed up the wave, then started spinning on it, big wooden oars flailing around. I scrambled to the high point, then had to scramble again each time the raft spun 180 degrees. I was like a hamster with his tail on fire, trying to get to the top of the hamster wheel before the whole mess of raft, metal frame, wooden oars and metal boxes flipped over into the hole. When that happens, it's the equivalent of being in a giant washing machine with all that gear. I wouldn't recommend it.

Though my days in churches are limited to times of marriage or death, I do know that there is a god somewhere in this world because my boat miraculously flushed out of that hole with me still in it, and the day ended happily.

For our second training trip, several days later, the water had come up to 8,000 cubic feet per second. This time, I had a fellow trainee in the front of my boat to add some ballast, albeit only 180 pounds. And since we had scouted the previous week, the group decided we didn't need to scout again. *Everyone knows where the hole is, right?*

Certainly.

When I hit the Gray's hole a second time, I knew what to expect. However, my passenger did not, and he was quickly sucked into the washing machine and disappeared downstream. As far as I know, he quit guiding shortly after that.

The third time I hit Gray's Grindstone—which, at this point, should have been renamed—the water was up to 10,000 cubic feet per second, and no shit, there I was. And again, the group agreed, no need to scout; *we all know where the hole is.*

When I hit the wall of water this time, the slant seat I was sitting on—3/4-inch wood—snapped in half. I was thrown high in the sky, landed in the hole, and started going round and round, a little cork in a giant surf. When I was pretty sure I couldn't take too much more, God reappeared, and I flushed out of the hole and into a maelstrom of rapids below. At that point, it was simply a swim for life.

For years as a kid, I swam on the Alpine Hills swim team. I never really liked it that much but for my friends on the team, and the coach, Steve Clark. Clark had been an Olympic champion and, more importantly to me at the time, just a nice guy. And he was the guy I thought of on my swim for life. He was the one that kept my head up and eyes on the shore, inspired my arm-over-arm water-polo swimming to safety, something you admonish guests never to do on a commercial river trip.

Safe on shore, I looked a hundred yards across the river—which might as well have been the North Sea—and saw Danny on the far side, rowing furiously, holding himself in the eddy. Then, in one of the more amazing feats of skill and strength I've ever seen, he ferried his boat across that rapid, 10,000 cubic feet of water every second trying to push him downstream. Somehow, he held his position even with me. When he got close, I did a Superman dive into his boat, and we flushed downstream to look for my sad little boat.

After three runs on the Tuolumne, I was now considered "trained up" and was turned loose with commercial guests. I don't think my outfitters truly knew the details of my "runs."

There are times when scouting a rapid, as distasteful as it is, can save your life, though not in the way you expect. A friend of mine, Dick Linford, recounts in the book "Halfway to Halfway" the story of when some of us—including Danny and Del mentioned above—ran a rapid on the Main Salmon called Whiplash. It was high water again: flowing over the gauge located in White Bird, Idaho, downstream of the rapid. This put the water flow somewhere between 80,000 and 100,000 cubic feet per second.

We had left our guests a mile upstream to get to a point where we could see the rapid safely. While we were mulling over the various options for getting through Whiplash—including lining our boats or portaging guest, boats and gear—when a group of private boaters came down river. They clearly hadn't scouted, and probably less clearly understood what they were rowing into. They each took a slightly different line, some in the general area that we had in mind, others more suicidal in nature. Three out of the five boats flipped. Gear and people were everywhere.

We were scouting from a point a couple hundred yards above the river, so we could be of no help to them. But they were certainly a help to us: five little lab rats that came along at just the right time. We all had clean runs.

I know this contradicts my impatience and penchant for hasty scouts, but, occasionally, if you wait long enough some poor bastard who doesn't know better will come along and just run it, sight unseen, usually in an eminently flippable cataraft. And you learn.

I don't recommend depending on the hubris of strangers to teach you a thing or two, but sometimes it does work out in your favor.

Why is scouting such a thorn in my side? Perhaps because it is a thinly veiled metaphor for one of the thornier questions of how to live one's life. In one ear is the voice of reason and parents and institutions: deny the moment, plan, be careful and deliberate, put life in the bank, so to speak. Draw it down later. Another voice chimes in the other ear, whispering: Pay attention to the now, live in the moment, grab life by the throat before it grabs you. Read and run.

Both my parents died in their early 60s of cancer, as did a dear friend in her 40s. Others get struck down by car wrecks and slip-and-falls before their lives have blossomed. I suppose those experiences bias me towards the latter philosophy, but not entirely.

I've run a lot of rapids over time and scouted more than I really wanted to. Getting perspective on the river, seeing the run-out of things can be helpful. Planning and seeing the line often works out well. But part of me accepts that once you leave the cliffy vantage of the scout and get back to river level everything looks different. The current is stronger here than there. Some rocks and holes are where you expect them, others aren't. Yes, you have some idea of what's coming, but often it reduces to sound and fury. Ultimately, you just go to make the move.

VII

On Guns and Hunting

Long days in the blind

I grew up duck hunting in Northern California. And even back then—mostly in the 70s—it was exactly that: hunting. There wasn't a lot of killing going on. Places like Grizzly Island and Los Banos looked the part; there just weren't that many birds. The reasons for that are varied and concerning, but, at the time, I didn't know any differently.

What became clear early on was that hunting was and would always be more of an aesthetic and social experience than anything else. Our trips generally began with a long drive to a rural, conservative farming area or other. We'd have dinner at a restaurant in town. As a 12-year-old, I didn't have long hair as some of my friends did, but I did sport a longish Glenn Campbell look. It wasn't a good look. Still, I was not prepared for the feeling I experienced when a waitress at an Italian place called Louis Cairo's asked my brother and me, "What would you two girls like to eat?"

Moments like these made it evident to me that hunting would entail entering a different but equally wondrous world of sorts. We'd sleep in an old trailer, get up in the cold, foggy dark and walk out to the duck blinds through ponds with quicksand-like mud. Once the sun came up, the beauty of the wetlands stretched out around us: a place of water and islands, tules and smartweed, hawks and cormorants.

For hours, in a barrel blind set in the ground, my dad and I would stare up at the sky looking for ducks. When the hunting was quiet, we would break our vigil to have chicken bouillon from a "Land of the Giants" thermos. It was time outside of time with my dad. He is gone now, but the thermos still sits in my kitchen cabinet decades later, albeit useless now.

On the rare occasion that I did kill a duck, it didn't bother me in the least. It bothered some of my friends back then—and probably even more of them now. "Bother" was, of course, a bit of a code word.

"Doesn't it bother you to kill something so beautiful?" was always the question. "And with a gun; it seems like an unfair fight."

On the latter point, I'm not so sure. Ducks are fast; they bob and weave, they fly high, in the fog, or just not at all. It's more than fair.

As to the former point, perhaps the best defense of hunting I have come across was made by the author Ken Kesey. His point, as I understood it, was that with hunting, at least, you must be conscious of the fact that something must die for you to eat it. Many times, as a child and adult, I have had to pick up a not-quite-dead duck from the pond and wring its neck until it was dead. And there was, subsequently, the plucking and the gutting, all by hand. It was and is a very visceral realization of what exactly is going on.

Conversely, picking up a skirt steak at the grocery store, you can blithely go about furthering your survival at the expense of some cow without the slightest thought as to what happened to that cow before it ended up in the shopping cart. While the meat packing industry has come a long way from Upton Sinclair's days, I'd venture to say that raising, killing, and processing cattle is still a fairly ugly proposition.

There is yet another argument to be made. If I kill an elk for food, is that less moral than that elk being killed by a wolf? The elk will be eaten by something; that is certain. Does it matter on the grand scale of morality what eats it?

Of course, vegans can easily dispense with arguments of both hunter and meat shopper. To that I would say: you win. However, I don't see the world's appetite for meat—whether due to evolutionary forces or just habits—going away anytime soon, if ever. On the other end of the spectrum, trophy hunters—those who kill not for meat but for wall hangings—don't have much of a moral foothold here at all.

Guns—for the most part—are implicit in hunting. So, hunters, myself included, certainly don't want the ability to "bear arms" to go away. The frustrating thing about the gun debate is that some gun rights proponents have come to see it as binary: that unless the right is absolute, it is somehow being taken away. But where else in life do we live in absolutes? Plenty of individual rights—free speech is an example—survive swimmingly with common sense boundaries to ensure the rights of the larger society.

For argument's sake, let's consider the Second Amendment absolute. Would my being able to buy and shoot a shoulder-mount rocket-propelled grenade launcher be reasonable, or desirable? I might get a boyish thrill in punching a hole in a hillside, but it doesn't seem like much of a thrill, or "right," to give up for the greater good of not having grenades exploding in the hills by my neighborhood.

Hunters and most recreational gun users realize that common sense has a place in life and that putting some boundaries on gun rights isn't going to make guns go away. The number of people who die in cars every year is comparable to those who die by firearms (roughly 37,000 – 40,000). Over the years, we have instituted all kinds of boundaries and rules regarding cars to lower the fatality rate. Cars don't even have the relative advantage that arms do in actually being specified in the Bill of Rights. Still, does anyone think cars are going away anytime soon?

While the debate rages, I hope more people get a chance to go hunting in some wild place. For the most part, hunting boils down to just spending time in beautiful country. You just happen to be holding a gun.

Hunting with a father or a son, a mother or daughter, or just a friend is an experience that simplifies a relationship, lets it build slowly, intricately, and with only the natural world bearing witness.

VIII

The Small World Duka

Finding humility before God

In the 1970s, the Small World Duka was what you would technically call a restaurant outside Nairobi. It amounted to some wooden picnic tables and a couple corrugated tin shacks plopped down on the expanse of the Kenyan plains. Farm animals—chickens, some goats, a few sad cattle—wondered around the place. There were no fences in sight and no apparent need for fences. The animals seemed to sense that they would fare better close to the Small World Duka than they would out in the wild world beyond. For the most part, they were right.

Brightening the scene was a giant Jacaranda tree that, when blossoming, would mark that drab spot on the plains with a shock of purple. In retrospect, I think the tree was the sole reason the Small World Duka was where it was. It threw shade over the picnic tables, giving patrons some relief from the sun while they ate.

Some of those patrons included my family and our African friends. We were living in Nairobi. My parents—a doctor and a nurse—were working in hospitals; my brother, Brion, and I were school kids, barefoot and feral much of the time, which, for us, was the beauty and whole point of being in Africa.

The little barbecue spot attracted Kenyans and ex-pats alike. My mom—much to my chagrin as a shy young boy—made friends with anyone and everyone she talked to. Put her in a room with a random sampling of society and she would come out friends with the one I was convinced was the axe murderer. So, our friends in Kenya cut across every distinction you could think of: tribal group—Luo, Maasai, Kikuyu—nationality, socio-economic status, age, and savoriness.

One hot afternoon we went to the Small World Duka with a couple of my parents' friends that I liked a great deal: Astrid, a Danish woman and Paul Kamau, a gregarious Kenyan who managed the Norfolk Hotel in Nairobi, an iconic hangout for the colonial set.

With cold beers on a table in the shade, my parents, Kamau, and Astrid launched into the politics of Kenya's fledgling independent state. None of it meant much to two young boys, so that was the cue for my brother and me to find something else to do.

We left the table and started wondering around the expanse of open land behind the tin shacks. The yard of the duka became savanna, stretching for all practical purposes forever. The field was littered with chickens and goats nibbling at the grass. Two little boys, younger than my brother and I, were chasing chickens, laughing as they ran. Brion and I joined them. One of the boys caught one at full sprint, then paid the price as the chicken gouged him on the hand with his beak. The boy threw the chicken up in the air, then sucked on the divot oozing blood from his hand. He and his friend exploded with laughter.

A few minutes later, two shirtless men wearing khaki shorts and sandals fashioned from tire treads walked out of the duka. They were speaking Kikuyu to each other. Goats and chickens scattered. They barked a few words to the boys we were playing with then spread out into the field, each with a long stick in hand. They singled out a goat—gray and skinny—and started herding it toward the boys. The boys, obviously skilled at this, moved to the flanks of the goat and ran alongside it as the two men behind flushed it forward. We followed the lot of them as they moved the goat into the back of one of the outbuildings.

It was not really a room as most would know one, just a space enclosed by three tin walls braced by tree branches. The dirt floor was hardened and shiny from use. A red sheet served as both the door and a fourth wall. There was some conversation in Kikuyu while the men fiddled with ropes. One of the men slipped a loop around the goat's neck then flipped the tail of the rope up and over a cross beam above us.

Before Brion or I really understood what was happening, the man with the rope yanked on it, tightening around the goat's neck. He heaved again and the goat lifted off the dirt floor. What sticks in my mind all these years later was the goat's frantic braying and dull, marble-like eyes staring out at the empty space. All that ended when the other Kikuyu man brought a big machete up to the goat's throat and cut it.

Kenya in 1970 was a wondrous place. Just a few years into its nascent independence, the country enjoyed the excitement and energy of a new democracy coupled with the infrastructure the British had left behind. There were schools and trains and commerce. The country was bursting with wildlife, occasional tourists, and a great deal of hope. Much of the country still lived an agrarian life, but it was an agrarian life in balance.

The upside of my mom befriending every questionable person we bumped into was that we came to know a lot of people. In addition to the ex-pats from Europe, we met Maasai elders, Kikuyu tribe members, Luo people, witch doctors, students, warriors, and duka owners. We were invited to a Maasai wedding and once a circumcision ceremony. They gave us celebratory drinks of cow's blood and milk, fed us meat from freshly slaughtered cows. We camped in the bush, hunted, crisscrossed the game parks, and more times than I can remember got our Land Cruiser stuck in the mud in places where we suddenly became the hunted instead of the hunters.

There could be no better place for a young boy to live and experience a wild world.

When that goat died, I was 10 but felt quite a bit older when later that day we had plates of barbecue ribs and ugali—a maize dish—the big sun dropping behind an even bigger horizon.

It was the first time I really made the link between my self— the needs and wants of a 10-year-old—and the rest of the world. That that goat died so that a handful of us could eat a meal was a truth that settled in, then took root. It marked a shift: The world wasn't just there for the taking, bounty provided by God—or some other facsimile—for us to gorge on. Actions had reactions;

they did not just happen in a vacuum. My 10-year-old brain suddenly saw the world as a zero-sum game. My gain came with the goat's loss. At the time, this was simply an observation as to the balance between life and death.

The concept reappeared in a different form later in life when I started studying science. In that setting, I came to know it as the law of the conservation of mass, which says in effect that in a closed system (our earth and sky) matter is neither created nor destroyed, but rather conserved. Matter can take different forms, but what we've got is what we've got. Ice can turn to water, which can turn to gas, but the world will always have the same number of hydrogen and oxygen atoms it has had since the beginning of time.

The same truism showed up later still while studying thermo-dynamics: energy is always conserved. It might transform from chemical energy (gasoline) to kinetic energy (moving car) to potential energy (car at the top of a hill), but the net amount is always constant.

It turned out that these two laws of nature were really the same thing. It took an Einstein—the actual one—to understand and illuminate the equivalence between matter and energy in the world's most famous equation that everyone knows but has a shaky understanding of ($E=mc^2$).

I bring this up not because people love to review high school physics but because the concept seems relevant to the trajectory of our lives. Like it or not, we are facing twin dilemmas: the world is heating up and the biodiversity of the earth is rapidly diminishing. Both are easily measured. And both, independently or together, can take us down.

What does the conservation of mass-energy have to do with the fate of the world?

Understanding and living by the principle of conservation precipitates a shift in perspective about our place in the world: from that of lording over a pantry of resources—separate and distinct from ecosystems—to one in which we are intimately connected to and dependent on the fate of other species and ecosystems. While over the course of evolution we have risen above all other species to dominate the earth, the fact remains that we need the rest of them to stay alive, let alone dominate.

Hunters, farmers, ranchers and Indigenous people—anyone who truly lives off the land—knows and lives this reality. You can't hunt if there is no habitat for what you hunt, can't farm if you deplete your soil. Overfish the salmon and your tribe starves.

Basically, you're doomed if you don't take care of your land, your animals, the habitats that they need.

The specifics of how biodiversity determines our fate could be the subject of a dissertation, and probably is. But the basics are simple. A diversity of species is critical to ecosystem resilience—we're talking about ecosystem or ecosystems on a grand scale—against perturbations, whether disease, dramatic climate shifts, or individual species extinctions.

Think of ecosystems as a game of Jenga. For the uninitiated, Jenga (derived from the Swahili word *kujenga*, to build) is a game developed in the early 1970s by a British woman living in Tanzania. Fifty-four wooden blocks, not all identical, are used to create a rectangular tower. Each player takes turns pulling one block out of the tower and placing it on top of the tower. Obviously, the tower can withstand a few missing blocks, but eventually it becomes unstable and collapses. Ecosystems behave the same way. There is stability—i.e., health—in numbers.

Healthy ecosystems represent much more than a tedious phrase you would find in a U.N. report. They generate the oxygen (through photosynthesis) and clean water (nitrogen uptake) and food (insect pollination—which generates one-third of the world's food production) that we need to live. What's more, a great many pharmaceuticals that keep us alive were first derived and continue to be harvested from natural sources.

We've been playing a big game of Jenga with the tower of species that keeps us alive. Since 1970 (right about when Jenga was developed), the population of vertebrates—mammals, birds, fish, amphibians and reptiles—has decreased by 68%. Invertebrates, the less charismatic creatures of the animal kingdom, are animals without a backbone—jellyfish, insects, parasites, fungi, corals, squids, among others. They comprise approximately 97% of all animals in the world, and their population has decreased by about 45% since 1980. The question is: At what percentage does the grand tower collapse?

As for climate, it is no great revelation to say that it is intertwined with our ecosystems. Mess with climate and you mess with a whole bunch of species at the same time and with unpredictable consequences.

The way I see it, the political fight over the cause of climate change—man made or natural—is a global waste of energy and time. What does matter is how greenhouse gases interact with solar radiation coming into our atmosphere and how they interact with the heat that leaves the earth (infrared radiation). The physics is thoroughly understood and demonstrable.

The second fact to note is that the amount of carbon and methane (the two worst greenhouse gases) in the atmosphere has increased dramatically since 1750 (we know this by analyzing air bubbles trapped in ice sheets over time). Does it matter whether those increases are a result of the Industrial Revolution or volcanoes? Fugitive gas leaks in coal and petroleum production or belching cows? Termites or concrete production?

We can argue about the past forever, but something we can control is the amount of carbon and methane we put in the atmosphere moving forward. We know that adding more exacerbates the problems we face; adding less reduces the problems we face. It's a basic closed system conservation of mass situation. We want to rebalance the carbon in our world—get more of it in plants and trees and in the earth and less of it in the atmosphere.

If none of this makes sense, then there is still another way to look at it. And that is through the lens of humility. I'm not a religious person, but I do know that humility before God—or whatever you deem to be God—is a central tenet in most religions. As it is written in the Old Testament: "Pride goes before destruction, a haughty spirit before a fall."

I don't know if humility will save humanity, but it's seems like a good way to start. Humility engenders respect and respect binds the world together.

I often think about that skinny four-legged fellow that died one hot afternoon in Africa. He's long gone now but, curiously, he sticks with me.

It's always surprising what you can learn from a goat.

IX

Flight of the Affluent

*Sometimes what's most dear is
left behind*

According to the United States Census Bureau, Stanley, Idaho, has a population of 69. The number seems a little suspect. On a July day, there could be 69 people in and around the town's gas station alone. In mid-January, with the temperature hovering at -10 F, you might think you were the last person on Earth, left to live your final moments in an empty Sinclair station. Apparently, someone in Stanley's 220-year history thought the place was too crowded and so decided to establish an Upper Stanley and a Lower Stanley. They are separated by perhaps a mile. The distribution of population between Upper and Lower Stanley is not known.

A river runs through both Stanleys. Actually, two rivers run through, though one is technically a creek. The other, the Salmon River, is a true river, a big Western river that runs to the ocean. If the fish for which the river is named make it to Stanley, they've come nearly 900 miles against the current. Most years, fewer than 69 make it. Sadly, those that do, don't know what they're missing just above the surface of the water.

The Sawtooth Mountains—at 30-50 million years old—are relatively young as mountains go. As the name suggests, the peaks are jagged and tower 3,500 feet over the town, which itself is well over a mile above the ocean from which the salmon begin their journey. Unfortunately, that's not all that looms over the town.

On the north side of Upper Stanley there is what looks like a bad mustache—a Brobdingnagian mustache of glass and steel—resting awkwardly on a cliff.

I bring it up not to highlight one spectacularly bad P&Z decision but because it is emblematic of what is going on across the West: The affluent are on the move.

With the leash of the corporate office cut, perhaps forever, droves of those with money and wherewithal are leaving otherwise pleasant places—San Francisco, Marin, Santa Monica, Seattle, Portland—and heading to the semi-rural West: Stanley; Bend; Bozeman; Sun Valley; Telluride; Flagstaff, Santa Fe; the list goes on. With that has come to these small Western communities the concomitant shortage of everything from affordable housing, day care, and classrooms, to fishing guides, e-bikes, shotgun shells, and sometimes hospitality.

Some of these are real problems and call in to question the sustainability of these now top-heavy Western towns. But this house—no doubt there are many of its ilk in every town I mentioned—concerns me for another reason.

What exactly does a house like that say to the thousands of summer visitors, 69 hardy residents, and fewer but even hardier salmon? Certainly, there is an element of financial flexing going on, but, really, who cares about that? Obtuse is a word that comes to mind; perhaps insensitivity to place and landscape. It also seems more than a bit disrespectful to those 69 people below who must look up at that thing every day, as if they were prostrate before some sort of lord.

Most importantly, though, it is a disavowal of community, which may be the biggest sin.

A sense of community is at the core of functioning society, but it is not something simply ordered up. It is ethereal, sometimes illusive and tends to develop organically through time and proximity and then trust. But once it is conjured, it becomes a force that can bind people who don't formally know each other, who are leading parallel lives that, while never intersecting, are close enough to be enjoyed and appreciated, even celebrated.

Recently, in the Wood River Valley of Idaho, where I live, a beloved woman, mother, athlete, and otherwise bright light recently died of glioblastoma. I didn't know her, but I knew her husband casually, on and off over the years. And I knew "of" her for 30 years. I don't know that we ever spoke. In tight communities, you can come to know someone, even feel close to them, without knowing them, just in hearing their names, or through conversations with mutual friends, or reading about their kids' soccer games or ski races in the local paper. So when this smiling woman appeared in an obituary photo one day, I stopped short. I had that sickening sensation of falling, when you're not sure where the bottom is. I could hardly read on.

A community is stronger than the sum of its parts. Conversely, when a part of that community falls away, the loss is greater than one. Oddly, it's personal.

In my little community, there has always been a tension between locals and non-locals. How long do you have to live in a place to be considered a "local," which is just another way to say, part of the community, part of the binding force? Is it five years? 10 years? 30 years? The truth is, none of us is really a local by the metric of time, except for a few Native Americans who happen to live here.

Maybe there is a simpler, more mundane way to answer that question. Do you find yourself leaning on the horn when some punk cuts you off, someone slides into the parking spot that belonged to you, or older person dithers at a stop sign? If so, as they say in the self-help world, you have more work to do. A local, in my estimation, would never use a horn to mete out his aggressions. Why? Because the person at the receiving end may very well be his neighbor, or son, or teacher, or mother of his daughter's best friend. In communities, there is accountability, a sense of others, and humility. Ultimately, it comes down to the fact that you care, care about those you know and even those you don't.

The stereotypical ethos of the West has been that of rugged individualism. Perhaps a stereotype, but nonetheless it is true: individualism courses through the culture of these places. What gets less notice but is just as true about the West is that there is a fierce and longstanding belief in community. Paradoxically, it is braided with individualism. The two strengthen one another. I suspect that in the days when you scratched a living from the earth here, you didn't make it without both. It's not clear if that's still true, but if I had a farm, I'd bet on it.

One thing still puzzles me about this house and the guy who is building it: What's he going to do when his kid kicks his soccer ball over that 200-foot cliff? I don't think his neighbor is going to just toss it back.

Maybe he needs a wall.

X

The Great Disruption

Living with uncertainty

The other day I went to a Christmas tree-lighting event at the town square. I was with my wife, youngest daughter, who is 3, and a hundred or so other people—some I knew; others I didn't.

It was what you would expect—carolers, hot chocolate, warming fires, a fire truck with the local Santa hopping out to greet children. There were cheery adults milling about with more than a fair share of small, scared children. Part of that angst I attribute to Santa. He scares a lot of small children. I remember my older daughter also being a bit leery of our Santa at the time, a beloved man named Jack Williams. I suppose if I were 3 feet tall and a corpulent, hairy old guy in a red pantsuit approached me, I'd be scared, too.

My daughter and several other 3-year-olds were clinging to their respective moms. But it seemed there was more to it than a scary old Santa. It occurred to me that these children were part of a generation of kids experiencing the world under the regimen of COVID-19. These are children who have started life without playdates, babysitters, trips to the market, in some instances even school—basically any significant social exposure. They are unsure of crowds, faces they don't know, events not carefully orchestrated for their safety.

Ironically, these COVID kids are living an ultra-controlled life due to an apparently uncontrollable pandemic. I find it a bit heartbreaking to watch a 3-year-old expertly don a face mask as a matter of course, and without complaint. This is now part of their collective lives.

It is also the rare experience for my generation, and now my children's, in which a threat—equally menacing to all—hangs over an entire population. It hadn't struck me until that tree-lighting event that I was a part of a generation that had mostly slipped through the cracks of historical upheaval.

I was born in 1960, and, with my cohorts, comprise the tail of the baby boom. We were born too late to experience the pall of WW II, the Great Depression, the Korean War and most of the Cold War. We were too young for Vietnam. And by the end of the 1960s, most of the childhood diseases were controlled with vaccines; smallpox, diphtheria, tetanus, pertussis, polio, measles, mumps, and rubella were of little concern to us. Chicken pox was about all we had to contend with. There was, of course, 9/11, and the wars that followed, but unless you lived in Manhattan or were in the military, that was an acute threat and one that became increasingly remote for most of the U.S. population.

I am no fan of wars, disease, or economic ruin. Still, I can't help but think that the generations before me were different because of these cataclysms—stronger, more resilient, burnished by humility and grace under pressure. Uncontrollable events have a way of revealing character.

Ushering people into the wilderness—as I did for many years as a guide—is hardly comparable to war and disease. Nonetheless, there is a lesson to be learned in wild places. I have noticed that as people float into a wilderness where pretty much anything can happen indiscriminately, their first reaction is to retreat into their established stations in life. But give them a few days in that world and they flourish. Strength, kindness, humility—real character—emerges.

I have a good friend who has, for years, been instrumental in the effort to build the future National Medal of Honor Museum in Arlington, Texas. A couple months back, he and a few of us toured the site and learned about the project and the medal itself, the first of which was awarded in 1863. It is the nation's highest award for acts of valor. To date, there have been 3,508 recipients (several have received it twice).

The character traits common to Medal of Honor recipients are courage and sacrifice, commitment and integrity, citizenship and patriotism. One could expend a lot of words and time debating what these qualities mean. For me, the thread running through all of them, though, is one of perspective. It is a manner of looking outward versus inward. It is acting for others, rather than for self. It is recognizing a bigger picture than what you see.

What defined the generations before me was their ability to not only survive but to thrive in a world riddled with uncertainty. While there have only been 3,508 Medal of Honor recipients in 158 years, the qualities those people embody have streamed through countless men and women who weathered battles of a different kind. Their first instinct was to reach a hand out, to imagine ways they could help the next guy before helping themselves. Aggregate that over a generation and remarkable things happen in dark times.

Now, suddenly, this generation that has escaped most of the great collective threats of the last century, finds itself facing a world that it hardly recognizes. The question hangs in the ether: how will we respond to the moment?

In the winter months, I work on a mountain. To get there, I park my car in a dirt lot, then walk about five minutes down a path and across a river on a bridge. Last week, I was walking to work; the night was inching towards day. As I crossed the bridge, a bald eagle flew over my head, close enough to startle me with the sound of his wings breaking through the cold air.

On one of my dad's last days before dying of cancer, he was in bed staring up through a sky light and spied an eagle high above. "That's where I would like to be," he said.

Even though I don't take much stock in events beyond the physical world, ever since that day I've always seen eagles as a visitation of some sort—a father gone from this world but still looking over his son. Maybe that's just what I wanted to believe.

Perhaps I had been inspired in Texas. Perhaps it was just the realization that the world had changed, but this visitation on the bridge was different. This was more of an invitation—from someone, or something—to behold others, to look outward not inward, to embrace the uncertainty sweeping the world, to ascend into the brightening sky and spread valor where it is needed.

Yes, you might fall from the great height. But then again, you might just catch the air right and soar. You might have a chance to glimpse that illusive place where the dawn sky meets the precious earth and an unscripted universe blithely unfolds.

XI

Getting in the Ring

When is it time to throw a punch?

I don't recall ever being in a real fight, the kind where you square off with someone and let rage call the shots. There were scuffles on the soccer and lacrosse fields, but that was in high school and college, and I was probably smart enough at that point to realize my average size and weight weren't going to win any real fights.

There were the ongoing battles with my brother. However, fighting your brother—which, in our battles devolved into more of a cartoonish WrestleMania than true fist-on-face violence— seems a bit like fighting yourself. The stakes are small, and the battles tend to be over distinctions without a difference.

In high school we had boxing in P.E. I remember being put "in the ring" against my friend Frank and feeling my first punch to the face. That didn't feel good, but it didn't engender the rage

I expected. What's more, it was all sanctioned as part of our education, if you can imagine that. It was clinical violence at best.

I do remember, vividly, my first experience with true malevolent violence. Years ago, I was in Manhattan for a meeting and went for an early morning run in Central Park. There was a misty rain falling. I remember because when I glanced down an alley, I saw a slick of blood on the wet pavement. It was pooled in front of a dumpster—yellow police tape cordoning the area. A dozen or so people were milling about, some in uniform, some not. It was so surreal I thought it must be a movie or TV shoot. But I lingered long enough to know it wasn't. Someone's life had ended there in the night. I tried to imagine what had transpired in those few moments before someone ended up in a dumpster. How could you get to a point where you could plunge a knife into someone and watch a life drain away? What in the world would you do with that memory?

The word violence gets used so in many contexts—"violent seas," "violent colors"—that its meaning gets diluted. At its roots —Latin and Indo-European—the word really means extreme force or aggression against others. Force on others.

For people fortunate enough to grow up without violence, the idea of becoming violent seems so far-fetched as to be fantasy. I sometimes wonder if there would ever be an occasion when I could be truly violent. Most parents can probably envision becoming violent if their children were being threatened by someone. Run through the thought experiment, and you'll feel rage —the fuel of violence—rise up for an instant.

It seems the Ukrainian War has supplanted COVID as the world's great tragedy. COVID was and is a tragedy almost antithetical to violence. There is no malice between it and others, no emotion to it. It is somewhat random in its path, more insidious than forceful.

The tragedy of the Russian invasion of Ukraine, on the other hand—so brazen and unabashed—is a much thornier tragedy. It raises the question of when, if ever, is it justified to use violence to stop a more depraved version of violence? Are there degrees of morality when it comes to violence?

Despite the reporting and documentation of what is transpiring in places like Bucha and Mariupol, the world as a whole really hasn't grappled with what is going on there: a maternity hospital being bombed, families cooking meat scraps over a fire in the rubble, mothers fleeing with toddlers in their arms and little else, people tied up, shot in the back of the head and left on the streets, mass graves, rape, torture, anarchy. They feel like scenes from another era, or they should be.

Putin is obviously a psychopath and will likely go down in history with others of his ilk: Stalin, Hitler, Mao Zedong, Pol Pot. But that does little good for people like the Ukrainian toddler Vira Makoviy. Her mother, Oleksandra Makoviy, fearing she and her husband would be killed by Russian troops, scrawled Vira's name on her back so that, should she be found alive, someone could piece together who she was.

I have a 3-year-old daughter who is in pre-school. I try to imagine being so desperate as to scrawl her name and birthdate on her back. Again, I come up with nothing. It's too remote; I can't conjure the situation to feel the emotion.

Occasionally, she will come home from pre-school confounded by the fact that another child had pushed her to get to a toy or climb the slide first. "Why did he do that, daddy?" she will say, eyes as big as the sun. There is in her voice the faintest hint of outrage, to the extent a 3-year-old can express outrage.

But then I wonder, what the hell is the matter with us? Surely, her instincts are right. Where is our outrage? Does not rape, torture, bombing of pregnant women, indiscriminate killing of civilians count for outrage? Granted, there is one big elephant in the room: the danger of provoking the use of nuclear or chemical arms. But given our remarkable technologies, the smarts and talents of our military, I have to believe there are multiple ways beyond economic sanctions to stop a psychopath. And yes, violence to stop the butchering of innocents is one of them. It's not a moral position I would brag about, but I think it is the right one floating in a sea of bad ones.

Perhaps hollow words from a guy who has watched the fights of his life pass him by, but some fights you have to take.

XII

Of Uranium and Armadillos

'Your tax dollars at work'

Early last spring, I spent some time at a backcountry ranch in the Northern Rockies. I was eating breakfast when a woman joined our table. She was very friendly and pleasant and, it turned out, a nuclear engineer at one of our 17 national labs.

Besides design power plants and bombs one hopes never explode, what does a nuclear engineer do? This one was trying to work out how to power a rocket to and from Mars with a small nuclear reactor.

Mars is, on average, 140 million miles away. The moon is less than a quarter of a million miles away. To get to the moon it took 13 years and $283 billion (adjusted for inflation), so this is no small problem for rocket scientists.

Towards the end of breakfast, someone else ambled into the eating area: a fellow who looked every bit the part of a coyote hunter. Turns out, he was a coyote hunter, part of the USDA's Wildlife Services program. Wildlife Services seems a somewhat ironic title in that a large part of the program's charter is to eliminate wildlife, specifically predators like coyotes, wolves, and foxes. Livestock Services might be more appropriate, as livestock (and their owners) are the primary beneficiaries of the program. To be fair, Wildlife Services also works to eliminate invasive species, identify wildlife diseases, and reduce aviation strikes and crop damage caused by birds. According to USDA reports, in 2020, Wildlife Services euthanized 62,537 coyotes and 381 gray wolves. Also eliminated were 790,136 European starlings, 113,331 feral swine, and 414 armadillos.

I suppose this could be the beginning of a belabored joke: "A nuclear engineer and a coyote hunter walk into a dining room …" Lucky for you, I gave up telling jokes decades ago after badly botching one in front of my high school drama class.

But this was a curious coincidence. How could these two people possibly have the same employer: the federal government? Still more questions came to mind. Why do we even have government? Should it provide everything from the aspirational (Mars) to the mundane (armadillo control)? And who should pay for it and why? In sum, the size and scope of government is a vexing debate in this country.

Our Declaration of Independence, which started all this, was an assertion of three seemingly simple ideas. One was that all "men" (and women) are created equal—a premise without which self-government, America's reason for being, is nonsensical. To make the point, in an imaginary democracy of 1,000 people, a king's vote could be apportioned a value of 999, and all his people given 1 vote. Would that constitute self-government, our ultimate goal in fighting the Revolutionary War?

A second assertion was that certain "natural rights," given to us by a notably undefined God, pre-existed all human laws. These were, of course, the right to "Life, Liberty, and the pursuit of Happiness." This provision was meant to trump any notion of the divine right of kings.

Finally, the Declaration asserted that governments, with the consent of its people, were created solely to "secure these rights."

So how did we get from securing natural rights to coyote hunters and Mars missions? It comes down to what you think life, liberty, and pursuit of happiness mean.

Life is easy; protecting us from foreign and domestic dangers seems straightforward.

Government securing our liberties gets a little muddier. Liberty, in the days of the Declaration, was understood to be freedoms that didn't deprive others of freedoms. It assumes we live in some sort of defined society and that one's actions can adversely affect others' ability to pursue life, liberty, and happiness. As Thomas Jefferson wrote, liberty is "... unobstructed action according to our will within limits drawn around us by the equal rights of others."

Part of the confusion today is that liberty is used interchangeably with freedom, the latter of which implies unrestrained actions. To provide a concrete example of the difference: Do I have the right to rebuff government-imposed COVID-19 public health measures—masks and vaccines—if, by breathing in your face at the check-out stand, I threaten your health and, potentially, your life? Traditionally, freedom says yes, liberty says no. This distinction has been lost over time.

"Pursuit of Happiness" is even more difficult to parse. At the time the Declaration of Independence was written, "pursuit," had a connotation less of seeking and more of attainment. Still, "happiness" is more problematic. Is it property? World peace? Health? Social justice? Or is it something else entirely that we have a right to attain? Everyone has a different idea of what it is. So, one of our "natural" and unalienable rights, what we fought for—"Happiness"—is about as subjective as it comes. It follows that what government should and should not be doing in securing it is inherently subjective too, and, therefore, fuel for political bonfires.

Saying big government is bad or big government is good is not good enough; we need to look at it in a more analytical way to gain any clarity on what we want. Size—absolute dollar amounts—and scope—the types of things government does—are the relevant parameters. But to complicate the puzzle more, the size of government expands due to structural reasons as well as with broadening scope. By structural, I am referring to the way our spending is fundamentally and legally organized, which is into three buckets: mandatory, discretionary, and interest on debt.

Mandatory spending—$3 trillion in 2020, according to the Congressional Budget Office (CBO)—basically comprises our social programs: Social Security, Medicare, Medicaid, and un-employment assistance. The dollar amounts of these cannot be set by Congress, only who is eligible and the largesse of specific benefits. With an aging population—more people drawing Social Security, fewer young workers paying in, and with more of the population with expensive health issues entering

Medicare and Medicaid—these programs by their very definition get bigger, all eligibility and benefit rules being constant.

Discretionary spending—$1.4 trillion—represents all other government programs, which Congress can and does control, including the military, education, transportation, and various other entities such as national labs and Wildlife Services.

Interest on debt—$0.4 trillion—is, well, interest on debt, which is created when we spend more than we take in with taxes for a given year.

So, almost 71% of $4.8 trillion of spending in 2020 was effectively not even up for debate as far as budgeting decisions go: 63% from mandatory items and 8% from interest payments due.

The structural effects on a ballooning budget over the last 60 years are easy to see in CBO graphs showing the relative spending on mandatory, discretionary, and interest items.

As a percentage of our budget, interest has been relatively steady, but mandatory spending has gotten much bigger and discretionary much smaller.

Clearly, unless eligibility rules and benefit packages are amended, both the dollar amount and the proportion of our total budget will continue to rise—barring any dramatic demographic changes—due to mandatory spending.

As far as scope goes, it is really controlled by Congress and its discretionary authority. Certainly, a wider scope of government —funding for euthanizing armadillos, for instance—will add to the size of our budgets, but nothing like what mandatory spending increases are and will be. So, reining in discretionary spending has an effect but only on about 30% of the budget.

I remember as a kid seeing big signs on the side of the road: "Your Tax Dollars at Work." These were good in one regard: Taxpayers could see with their own eyes what exactly they were buying with their hard-earned tax dollars. Unfortunately, those job sites invariably had more than their fair share of guys leaning on shovels smoking Marlboros. Beyond bad public relations, this scene speaks to the twin Achilles heels of government: inefficiency and accountability. Without accountability there is rarely efficiency. Likewise, as projects (and governments) get big, they get inefficient; and when they get inefficient, accountability gets lost in the construction dust.

It is true that private markets are often more efficient than governments in solving problems. Unfortunately, they don't work in every situation. We, as a society, might value certain things that private industry has no vested interest in addressing. Put another way, if the cost or value of something doesn't appear on a company's income statement, why would they consider it? It's what an economist would call an externality. There are many of them out there, but one obvious example is long-term clean air and water. Generally, we all need it to live, but no single private entity has the specific financial incentive to address it.

So, what is the right size of government? Justice Potter Stewart once addressed a different subjective question—what is "hard-core pornography?"—by famously saying, "I know it when I see it ..."

Maybe. However, when the size of government next comes up for debate, before answering reflexively, it's worth asking a few pointed questions: What exactly do you want from government? And why? And at what cost? Perhaps most importantly, what exactly does happiness mean to you?

Some guys love a good coyote hunt; others like the idea of little bombs carrying us to distant places.

XIII

Living in the Land of Why

*Words make
the world go 'round*

Spend a little time with a 2-year-old and you'll find your conversations often go something like this:

"Why are we stopping?"

"Because there is a stop sign."

"Why is there a stop sign?"

"So the cars can take turns going through the intersection."

"Why is there an intersection?"

"Some people want to go this way, and some people want to go that way."

"Why do some people want to go that way?"

And so you go down a rabbit hole of Lewis Carroll's fancy.

I've been through the experience with three children now. People often shrug it off as a "phase," a word that implies that this dizzying and sometimes exhausting questioning goes away after a while. I don't think it ever really goes away; it just becomes less vocal, more internalized, as we age.

What's curious is that somewhere in those young brains is an intuitive understanding that the world is a rational one. Whether this sense is learned very early on or is inherited isn't clear. What is clear is that our perception of the world—at least when we start out—is that, however mysteriously, things are connected by reason. Sometimes the path from A to Z is neither linear nor obvious—there might be some turns left and right along the way—but each turn leads inexorably to Z.

To face the unremitting question why—and to just as diligently try to answer those pesky questions—can feel a bit like being trapped in a Beckett play. But, if we really do suppose that we live in a rational world, asking why is our best tool for moving forward in it.

Why is the sky blue?

Because blue light is preferentially scattered by the molecules in the atmosphere.

Why is blue light preferentially scattered?

Because it has the shortest wavelength of the light we can see.

Why does blue light have the shortest wavelength?

Because it has the highest frequency.

Why does it have the highest frequency?

Because the speed of light is constant and equals the product of a wavelength and frequency. Wavelength and frequency are like two ends of a teeter-totter; if wavelength is small, frequency has to be big.

Why is the speed of light constant?

Ask Einstein.

The relentless drilling down to truth that children do intuitively and that adults sometimes have to relearn is our engine for understanding. It forces us to wonder: Why exactly do we do this or that? What do we really believe? What is the right thing to do?

What parents quickly learn from their children is that they had better choose their answers and, more specifically, their words very carefully. Why? Because the actual words you choose lead to the next question. Get careless with your words and before you know it, you'll find that that rabbit hole leads to pretty philosophical, sometimes awkward questions and inconsistent answers.

I once interviewed now retired Supreme Court Justice Breyer, and he, too, taught me some things about words and the value of asking why. I met him at a pond outside the hotel where he was staying for a conference. He arrived alone, on a bike, in a t-shirt and swimming trunks. Apparently, he had just gone swimming in the river nearby.

We talked for over an hour about a lot of things, but he kept coming back to the importance of words and the value in understanding the "intent and purpose"—the why—behind them.

He characterized his work on the Supreme Court this way:

"The job requires us to look at works on paper, sometimes the Constitution, sometimes statutes. And those words are in front of us, and the question is what do they mean, and how do they apply in the particular case because lower court judges, in similar cases, applying these same words have come to different conclusions."

But drilling down to a truth does not mean simply looking up words in a dictionary. The answer is not there. For example, he explained, "Usually, the word 'liberty' is not a problem; that is, understanding the word. What is a problem is understanding the scope of the phrase that uses the word 'liberty' in the 14th Amendment (due process and equal protection of the law) ... So, you look at the history of the phrase, to the tradition, the context, purpose—somebody wrote those words, what was their intention? And consequences as viewed through the lens of their intentions."

Not everyone subscribes to this emphasis on intent. Breyer noted that his late colleague, Justice Scalia, whom he affectionately called "Nino," was loathe to consider purpose and intent. His fear was that it would invite subjective interpretations of the Constitution.

Breyer's retort to Scalia was that if he relied solely on the text —the what and not the why—rulings would be too restrictive. "This is a document that is supposed to affect how people live over a long period of time," he said. "Really, it's his (Scalia's) view that he wants clear rules. And he will work pretty hard to get a clear, general rule. But I'll say sometimes it's dangerous to have a rule because situations come up that you never thought of, and it will hit you in the face."

Ultimately, Breyer said, their difference was in "temperament and degree. He's more comfortable with rules ... I'm more willing to live with a mess." The two were on the bench together for 22 years.

That "mess" could be crudely defined as democracy at work. As he put it: "We try out all kinds of things, then we scream at each other, then we try out some more things, maybe in an administrative rule, maybe in a state law, maybe in a federal law, or agreement. Then we change things. It's a learning process, and we'd like to hope it works toward the better ... The Court works best when it comes in at the end of the process to say ... not whether the solution is the best solution, but whether the solution is within the bounds that the Constitution sketches. Because that's what the Constitution does, it's a set of boundaries. It doesn't tell people what to do. It tells them what are the limits on their deciding for themselves of what to do."

That's a tall order for a document comprising only 7,591 words—words that, evidently, were chosen very carefully. In 230 years, they have been changed only 17 times. They have, however, been challenged thousands and thousands of times. Generation after generation of children and judges keep probing, asking why, then why again, always seeking the truth in our experience.

All of this reminds me of a math puzzler a teacher posed to our high school class one day, many days ago. You are in San Francisco, and you plan to travel to New York. If you travel half the distance to your destination each day, how many days does it take to get there?

The answer is, of course, you never get there. But you do get closer.

XIV

Cow vs. G5

And other thoughts on a hot day

I have a young daughter who loves jets. And by jets, I mean just about anything that can fly. Single engine props, gliders, commercial airliners, and private jets all fall into the category of "jets" by her accounting. That's my fault; early on I decided it was just an easier word for her to learn than a panoply of terms: airplane, prop plane, turbo prop, and so forth. Regardless of nuance, they all hold a fascination for her, and me, I suppose.

So, on Daddy days, we often ride a bike down to the local private airport to watch the jets come and go. The modest entrance to the airport is a one-and-a-half-lane road. On one side is a fence lined with big fancy jets: G5s, Learjet 60s, and Citations. On the other side is a fence holding back a few hundred cows— brown ones—that's how much I know about cows. But if cows could spit, they could hit the tail wings.

The juxtaposition of the two is a bit surreal—new world and old world—but not all that unusual for a place like Idaho. The oddity did make me wonder one day: what's worse for the atmosphere—a G5 or a cow? This idle thought was no doubt spurred by the fiery hell of a summer everyone in the West was suffering through at the time. Somedays it felt like we were living on the surface of the Sun.

Running the gauntlet between jets and cows that day, I realized I really didn't have a great grasp on climate change, greenhouse gases, and the overall fate of the world. This was a bit shameful because I was a chemical engineering major in college. However, I figured that if I was a little fuzzy on one of the bigger debates of our lifetime, then chances are others might be, too. I, at least, owed it to my professors—particularly Professor Acrivos who taught me everything I know about heat transfer—to better understand what everyone is getting so hot about.

Planetary scientists like to call Earth the "Goldilocks" planet. As you may or may not remember from the fairy tale, Goldilocks—lurking about in the cabin of the three bears—finds three bowls of porridge: one too hot, one too cold, and one "just right." Earth, too, is not too hot and not too cold, but just right. Why? Because when the heat coming into our world from the Sun balances with the heat going out to space, we happen to end up at an average equilibrium temperature (59 F) that enables liquid water to exist, without which we wouldn't exist.

When thinking about this big heat transfer problem, the first thing to realize is that we're talking about an exchange between only two entities: the Sun is one and the Earth/atmosphere is the second. Our atmosphere and Earth are intimately connected.

One might think that the atmosphere is just air that blows around and doesn't have much to do with us. But because of gravity, our atmosphere is always attached to us. It's kind of like the cloud of dust that follows Charlie Brown's buddy, Pigpen, around, only it's not dust but a bunch of gases all mixed up. Most of it is oxygen and nitrogen (99%), elements also crucial to life for processes like breathing, photosynthesis, DNA, RNA, and such, but not relevant here. Only 0.1% of the atmosphere comprises what we call greenhouse gases: water vapor, carbon dioxide, methane, ozone, nitrous oxide.

The Sun bombards us with solar radiation. Some of that energy gets reflected back to space before it gets to us, some is absorbed by the atmosphere on the way in, but most of that energy sails right through the atmosphere and is absorbed by the land and water on Earth. And just like an asphalt parking lot that radiates heat at night when things cool off, so does the Earth as a whole.

But—and this is what the heat transfer test would hinge on if there were one—because the Earth is at a different temperature from the Sun (59 F vs. 9,941 F) the energy returning to space is at a different wavelength from the energy that came in. And because of that subtle fact, a lot of the energy radiated from the Earth is absorbed by greenhouse gases in the atmosphere rather than just sailing unimpeded back to space.

What does absorbed mean? The energy excites the greenhouse gas molecules in the atmosphere. They vibrate and move around faster—kind of like giving a kid a chocolate bar. The average temperature goes up.

This weird wavelength shift causes the atmosphere to work like a one-way filter: the energy comes into our world unimpeded, but not as much is able to get out. Happily, that works out for us because after the energy-in and energy-out balance, the temperature settles at 59 F. If we didn't have the naturally occurring greenhouse gases up there to prevent some heat from going back to space, the temperature on the Earth would balance out at a much colder and inhospitable 0 F.

So, what's the problem?

Basically, it comes down to where the carbon is.

Our world—Earth and atmosphere—has always had the same amount of carbon in it, and always will. That carbon is in rocks and fossil fuels underground, in the plants and trees (cellulose), in living organisms (proteins, carbohydrates, fats), and in oceans (living organisms, calcium carbonate, and gases in the water). We are running into trouble because since the Industrial Revolution we have been redistributing that carbon—moving it from the ground (fossil fuels) and plant life and into the atmosphere in its gaseous forms (carbon dioxide and methane, for example). With more of these gases in the atmosphere, more heat is absorbed by them, and so our average temperature here climbs a bit.

Venus is sometimes called our sister planet, mostly because it is our neighbor in the Solar System and has a similar size and density. However, it is not a Goldilocks planet. Its atmosphere is 96% carbon dioxide—a sort of end game scenario for Earth. When your atmosphere has that much carbon dioxide in it, very little of the Sun's inbound energy escapes from it, and the temperature climbs. The ambient temperature on Venus is about 900 F, which makes our summers look pretty good.

Now back to cow versus G5. In 2019, the U.S. added a lot of greenhouse gases to the atmosphere, as we do every year. In essence, we took a lot of carbon containing compounds from the ground, plants and trees; used them for one thing or another; and put the end product of all those uses—14.5 trillion pounds of carbon dioxide—back into the sky.

Where do all these emissions come from? By economic sector, it breaks down to approximately 29% from transportation, 25% from electricity (generation), 23% from industry, 13% from commercial and residential, and 10% from agriculture. Hidden in these numbers are the G5s and the cows.

A G5 burns kerosene at a rate of 400 gallons per hour. At the end of that hour, it has dumped approximately 8,500 pounds of carbon dioxide into the sky.

Now, the lowly cow. You wonder, what could she possibly be doing wrong?

Cows are unusual animals—they are ruminants—which means they have a special stomach that enables them to ferment their food. What's the byproduct from fermenting all that grass (cellulose/carbon)? Methane, one of the most effective greenhouse gases when it comes to trapping heat. How do cows get rid of all that methane? Not what you think. They burp it out.

Each year, an average cow belches out 220 pounds of methane, which is 28 times more potent than carbon dioxide as far as absorbing heat. Do the math and you get the equivalent of 6,160 pounds of carbon dioxide per year.

A cow left alone might live 20 years, but they aren't, of course. In reality, a dairy cow is allowed five years of burping, a beef cow two years. So, we're looking at a maximum of roughly 31,000 pounds of carbon dioxide emitted during the life of that cow, less than four hours in the G5.

Head-to-head, the cow wins the green award.

Unfortunately for the cow, if you lump her together with all her bovine friends they out-belch all the private jets by almost 50-fold.

Doesn't seem like a fair fight, does it?

XV

Ode to Place

The case for conservation

I did not know Senator Frank Church, but several years ago I did spend one afternoon talking with his wife, Bethine. She was a lovely lady: smart, thoughtful, warm, someone who sends you a handwritten thank you note for visiting, even though she was the host.

I had gone there to talk to her about her late husband, a man who, as a Democrat in the staunchly Republican state of Idaho —then and now—was reelected three times, serving a total of 24 years in the Senate (1956-1980). While Church focused much of his time in the Senate on foreign affairs, perhaps his most profound mark on America was his work in conservation. Church sponsored two bills that have had and will have effects long after any of our lives: the Wilderness Act of 1964 and the Wild and Scenic Rivers Act of 1968. Late in his senatorial career, Church was also instrumental in employing the former law to protect an enormous swath of the Northern Rockies—2.4 million acres—

which now bears his name: the Frank Church–River of No Return Wilderness.

Most people in the U.S. have not seen this place, nor will they. It is rugged, distant, sometimes forbidding. But they should; a place like the Frank Church Wilderness changes people.

I suspect that most of us have a place, maybe two or three, that forms his character as much as parents and friends do. For me, that was Africa—I lived there as a child—and the Frank Church Wilderness. I have spent a good chunk of my adult life in the latter—guiding people down the rivers that run through it on their way to the Pacific.

I've often wondered what it is about wild places that is so compelling? For one, entering a place like the Frank Church Wilderness demands giving up control—control of everything— which is sometimes exactly what we need. It is to enter a world in which the scale of time and physical dimension dwarfs anything we are familiar with. The Middle Fork of the Salmon drainage, for instance, which runs through the heart of the wilderness area, is estimated to be 2 million years old. People have been in that area for perhaps 8,500 years—which means for 1,991,500 years—life, death, change, and growth moved along swimmingly in that canyon without even an inkling of us.

I've seen it happen hundreds of times: men and women— forces in finance or politics or the arts—enter a place like that with swagger and hubris. But within a day or two, they have shed all that. They are humbled and awed by the scale of things. Rather than the stars of their own universe, they become observers, happy extras in a much bigger drama.

Then there is the beauty. Places in the natural world for which we feel affinity are often deemed "beautiful." But what exactly makes them beautiful, and why does that resonate with us? What makes a cliff band more beautiful than the face of a skyscraper?

For me, the beauty resides in simplicity. The natural world is stripped down to basics: rocks, trees, soil, water, life, death. There are no human constructs like politics, money, or social stratification overlaid on it, constructs that can complicate our experience.

Some people equate simplicity with stasis. But spending time in wild places, one can't help but sense he is in the real action of the world, that—albeit impossible—you are witnessing evolution at play. It is raw life unspooling, and there is a beauty in that.

After reading Darwin's, "On the Origin of Species," Henry David Thoreau, one of America's first naturalists said: "The development theory implies a greater vital force in Nature, because it is more flexible and accommodating, and equivalent to a sort of constant new creation."

For anyone looking for religion in nature, there it is. And this from a guy who worked in a pencil factory.

That the Middle Fork of the Salmon has been snaking through the Idaho Batholith—an enormous granitic mass—for 2 million years and will likely be doing the same for another 2 million years is somehow comforting. It places us right in the middle of a seemingly endless arc of time. Some might consider that a sad blip of existence. I find it reassuring for some reason, that life carries on, even if it is not mine, nor my kids', nor their kids'. It is a reality that imparts structure and stability to our otherwise mercurial existence in the civilized world.

Finally, there is the indifference. Go to a place like the Frank Church Wilderness and one can't help but feel its indifference to human machinations of wish and whimsy. There are no judgements, prejudices; there is absolutely no subjectiveness in the natural world. It just is. And that is refreshing.

The irony of that indifference is not lost on me. Our connection to place wouldn't be as deep without our human experiences there. I can't go around a corner of the Middle Fork without thinking of a friend, a guest, something that happened —good or bad—in the past. They are all ghosts now. Some have died, others have moved on to different lives, others have just vanished. It is true, as Thomas Wolfe famously titled one of his novels, "You Can't Go Home Again." However, sometimes a place can evoke memories and senses such that the very essence of past experience can feel real—as if it were still happening. It is fleeting, but it's undeniable.

Several years ago, I was on the big island of Hawaii running along a beach. When the sand ended in a rocky outcrop, I followed a trail inland and found myself in big open fields of tall dry grass and thorny trees. The air was drier than it was on the water. There were no houses, just an expanse of open land. I can't explain it logically, but something about the smell of the grass and trees, the texture of the air, the spread of land in front of me—the feel of that place—conjured for me a very different time and place. I suddenly felt exactly as if I were in Kenya as a child—on the wide plains—a place I loved dearly and had lived as a 10-year-old decades earlier. It was so real and true to my memory; I just wanted to keep going, to hold that feeling a little bit longer. Every day I went back to that place, and I got the same rush of memory, that same feeling of connection. It was like a drug I couldn't get enough of. When I ran back down to the beach each day, the feeling vaporized.

That deep yearning reminds me of a passage from another book, "The Sheltering Sky," by Paul Bowles. In it, Kit is recalling something her husband, Port, had said before he knew he was dying of typhoid fever:

"Death is always on the way, but the fact that you don't know when it will arrive seems to take away from the finiteness of life. It's that terrible precision that we hate so much. But because we don't know, we get to think of life as an inexhaustible well. Yet everything happens a certain number of times, and a very small number, really. How many more times will you remember a certain afternoon of your childhood, some afternoon that's so deeply a part of your being that you can't even conceive of your life without it? Perhaps four or five times more. Perhaps not even. How many more times will you watch the full moon rise? Perhaps twenty. And yet it all seems limitless."

Perhaps, it's a bit of a morbid sentiment. But as people go through life, they reach a tipping point when those thoughts enter their minds unbidden. I can't say it's unhealthy, just unsettling. But if you gird yourself for it, it can also be exhilarating: to look at things as if it were the last time you were going to see them.

Senator Church lived a relatively short life, only 60 years. He died of pancreatic cancer in 1984. On that warm afternoon having tea with his wife, I realized that Frank Church had understood the poignancy that resides at the intersection of our mortality and the exquisite beauty of a limitless natural world. Bethine recalled to me her husband's dying, which was a protracted affair. Just a few weeks before his death, though, he was told that the River of No Return Wilderness would be named in his honor as the Frank Church-River of No Return Wilderness. He said to his wife of 37 years, and friend for many more: "It was worth dying so long for."

XVI

Imaginary Friends

Who would you conjure?

When my son was a toddler, we had a tough time keeping clothes on him. As cute as his clothes were no doubt, he just didn't like being encumbered by it all. I could relate, I suppose, but that wasn't an option for a dad.

The rub was that we lived and still do live in the mountains. So, for a good part of the year, his need to be free expressed itself in the winter wonderland of our backyard.

I marveled at his ability to play in the snow totally naked. Of course, I was concerned, too. But every parent starts out with the intention of being above God's reproach; that quickly dissipates. Compromises are made, deals struck to keep the peace. So, my boy played naked in the snow. Everybody was happy.

One day when my guilt got the better of me, I went outside to check on him. I found him deep in conversation. Granted, kids are masters of the non sequitur and confusing word choices, but if you look closely, you'll usually find a pretty clever thread of logic that traces back to something you said hours earlier.

Not this time. He was having a perfectly logical conversation—
it seemed—it just wasn't with me. It was with somebody who
clearly was not there, clothes or no clothes.

This was my first experience with imaginary friends.

My second experience came during another instance of
questionable parenting. On a whim, I had decided to take
my oldest daughter on a hike to a mountain lake. She was 5,
maybe 6. Norton Lake was 5 miles away, and uphill, as mountain
lakes tend to be. But, with her usual Buddha-like equanimity,
she trekked along without a complaint. We had lunch, splashed
around in the sky-blue lake and took a little rest in the sun.

It wasn't long, though, before a gloom came over me. It
settled in my stomach—an unruly knot of fear and desperation
and guilt that parents get when they realize they have done something monumentally stupid with their child. I had overlooked
the most basic axiom of the mountains: climbing up is the easy
part, getting down is the rub. Forget that on Everest and people
die. God knows what happens when you do that with a 5-year-
old on a day hike.

That's when I met Diamond and Rainbow. It seems these
were two horses—splendid ones, no doubt—with whom my
daughter was, apparently, well acquainted. Somehow fathoming
the predicament her father had put her in, my daughter wrangled
up Diamond and Rainbow and rode them all the way down the
mountain—5 long miles. It was a miracle—circus-like, but one
that got my daughter down to our car and dad off the hook for
endangering his daughter.

Then there is Dewey. She is the imaginary friend of my youngest daughter. Dewey is a baby, but I have to say, a little menacing. Dewey is often pushing or kicking my daughter. Dewey sleeps a lot. She joins us for dinner but misbehaves. She doesn't share very well. More than once, I thought it might be time to drop Dewey off on the steps of the local fire station. But lately, I've warmed to Dewey.

Of course, the first—my son's—imaginary friend scared the hell out of me. When adults start to converse with the ether those around them start whispering words like schizophrenia and psychosis. Sadly, my parents—both medical people—were not alive to ask about this new development in our family, nor was Google then the magical font of knowledge it is today. I had, however, remained friends with a few of my dad's medical school buddies who had become psychiatrists. They quickly put me at ease about the imaginary friend. They told me it was normal, maybe even a good thing. So, I embraced the newest member of our family, and those who were to follow.

Little did I know at the time, but scientists were studying imaginary friends and other developmental stages children experience on the way to social intelligence and what's called "theory of mind," a concept first formulated by Simon Baron-Cohen, Uta Frith, and Alan Leslie in 1985.

Theory of mind is not something we are born with, rather we develop it at a young age. And it is crucial to our ability to interact socially. It is an ability to recognize beliefs, knowledge, and emotions—essentially any mental state—in ourselves and others. What's more, a child who has developed theory of mind is able to understand that his or her mental state—knowledge of something or belief, for example—may differ from that of someone else.

An often-cited experiment to see if a child has developed theory of mind is a false-belief task such as the Band-Aid box and pig figurine test. A child is shown a Band-Aid box and asked what he thinks is inside. Most likely he will say Band-Aids. Then that child is physically shown that inside the box there is actually a pig figurine, not Band-Aids.

Next, a second child enters the room who hasn't seen inside the box. The first child will be asked what he thinks the second child will say when asked what's in the box. If his response is "pig" it is evident he has not developed theory of mind; it is inconceivable to him that someone could believe something different from what he knows to be true.

A child who has developed theory of mind will respond "Band-Aids," understanding that the second child thinks there are Band-Aids in there, even though there are not. It is a measure of a child's understanding that someone else may believe something not only different from him, but that conflicts with reality.

What is not imaginary in the world today are the pitched battles we find ourselves in: red-blue, rural-urban, vaccination-no vaccination, health mandates-no health mandates, climate change-no climate change. And it strikes me that the parallel universes that have formed are partly due to our own failings. What we once fathomed as children—that others could believe something different from us, even if it were untrue—has somehow fallen from our understanding. It strikes me that theory of mind might just be the precursor to empathy, an emotion that we seemed to have collectively misplaced. Perhaps it is simply floating listlessly offshore in our minds, sort of like the hundreds of container ships off the coasts of Long Beach, Louisiana, New Jersey—all waiting to be found in the great supply chain breakdown of 2021.

As far as I know, I've never had an imaginary friend. But I have had an imaginary conversation. Many years ago, I was on a plane to Las Vegas, witnessing a little drama that was a middle-aged woman who had clearly availed herself of everything Las Vegas has to offer—big hair, Botox, gobs of makeup—trying to pick up a 19-year-old college student sitting next to her. Before I knew it, a friend—who was no longer alive—and I were in a humorous banter back and forth, silently, I think and hope, about this unlikely coupling, their future love children, and further adventures.

I do know at one point that I did laugh out loud, so then I was the lunatic on the plane. But what was so startling in retrospect is that the entire conversation was spontaneous—everything my friend said just sprung forth in my mind as if she were thinking it and saying it at that moment. There was never a moment of consciousness speaking to me: "This is what Kelly would think and say." She just said it.

It was weird and unexplainable but thrilling in a way. It has never happened since.

No doubt our brains conjure things for a reason. Perhaps we need to puzzle through a problem, weigh our feelings about an issue, or maybe just have a laugh with an old friend. Too often we dismiss the conjuring. There can be wisdom there.

Musing about imaginary friends made me wonder what it is we seek in our real friends. No doubt, everyone has a different answer to that question; what comes to mind are fortitude, wisdom, compassion, trust, or maybe just endurance.

I started at the very beginning and pondered the people who have been either at my side, or right there in my mind's eye for a lifetime: some from kindergarten, others from sports teams, high school and college, guiding, ski patrolling, the writing world, other professional experiences. Some I haven't seen for years, and may not for many more, or ever. But good friends, I've learned, carry on a relationship as if you never left.

The thread that tied everyone together was humor. To a tee, my friends have made me laugh. If you make me laugh and I make you laugh, then there's a pretty good chance we'll be friends. Doesn't matter too much if you think there's a pig in that Band-Aid box or not.

After I had this little epiphany, I felt a bit shallow, like all of those grand qualities—fortitude, wisdom, compassion, trust, endurance—were lost on me. I don't think they are. But, in the end, humor for me has always been the wellspring of joy. And joy is really the final currency. Take away that, and we're doomed.

XVII

The Long Stare

When it's time to go

Certain words in the English language are just inherently un-interesting. Interesting, for one, is a dolt of word. Another word that strikes me as a bolus of Novocaine to the brain is retirement.

While interesting is a word with little or no connotations attached to it, retirement, on the other hand, is a dull word with schizophrenic connotations. Some would say it connotes warm days on the golf course, long lunches, and naps in the shade. Others see it as a little more sinister, something akin to a stay at a CIA black site. I tend to fall in the latter camp.

It makes me somewhat uneasy when I hear people pining for retirement—visualizing it as some sort of secular Holy Grail grasped after a life of toil. That calculus might work well for a Sandals marketing campaign, but it falls short as a way to lead a life. Whatever we do, retired or not, has to have some meaning, stir some passion, or connect us to something, otherwise we are lost.

Maybe you can get connected to a sunset on a Florida beach, but it seems like a transitory joy—not one you can really take to your grave. And it could be that the Holy Grail is less a destination to be reached than a quest unto itself— a life of fits and starts, turns left and right, in search for what makes you happy and, hopefully, does some good for others around you.

Retirement has been on my mind—not for personal reasons —but because over the last couple of years, I have had three friends retire from a job and life we have all shared for decades. We ski patrolled together—a job with little glory, less money, and virtually no upward mobility. But I know we all loved it.

While it used to be the norm, these days it seems a rarity for people to work together in a job for decades on end. We, on the other hand, spent hour upon hour, day after day, year after year, together in an old log shack perched at 9,000 feet. In that monastery of sorts, a job morphs into a family, and a way of life, and through sheer force of time gathers meaning. I think of the innocuous facts I've learned about these longtime co-workers. They are tics and habits, nuances of speech, instincts and skills they possess, words they tend to use, views peculiar to each of them. Whether you find those tics and nuances annoying or endearing is irrelevant; they form a sort of scaffolding for friendship. Over time they harden and solidify. A similar braiding of lives happens in fire stations and military units, and, of course, marriages. The little things bind us together over time.

I don't think it matters what you actually do, but do something for years and years and it acquires an inherent value. And so, the ending of it comes with anguish. Leaving it is like leaving a family or being exiled from your homeland. Sounds dramatic, perhaps. But I've seen the realization wash over friends, and it is dramatic. It comes in the guise of the long stare to some middle distance. What they see and feel is hard to know. I would guess some longing, fear, uncertainty, maybe acceptance.

What I do know is that life's poignancy comes with the finiteness of our days, whether we are talking about our life's work, or simply our lives. And we all desire relevance in the world's affairs, however big or small. Once we retire, the cold truth is we cease to be relevant to the current state of affairs. We might have been pillars of an organization, built it, shaped it, but the fact remains—the instant we step away we will be irrelevant in a place for which we were relevant for decades. What I've come to appreciate about my friends' experience over the last few years is that that is a profound reckoning to accept.

Perhaps part of the appeal of retirement is that we sometimes fantasize about going out in dramatic fashion. I spent years as a commercial river guide and still do the occasional trip. But, for whatever reason, I have always envisioned my exit from that world. When it was time, I would position my boat mid-stream, offer a wink and a nod to my guests, ship my oars, and dive into the water. The swim to shore would be brisk and clarifying, the hike out of the wilderness the purest taste of freedom.

Drama or no drama, the problem always lies in the end. Ski patrolling, the line of work that I have shared with these three friends, is physical and often unfolds in rough weather and rougher terrain. More often than not, the physical demands of the job end it for you. You can't always dictate when you quit.

Other professions have similar roadblocks: a surgeon who loses his steady hand is no longer a surgeon, a computer engineer with failing logic fails to be a computer engineer.

None of my friends who retired, really wanted to. They wanted to keep going—but, I think, they wanted to keep going less for the job itself and more for the camaraderie— the little moments of humor and friendship—and a connection to something bigger than self.

What I have come to know about the long stare is that retirement—this tiresome construct of the First World—presents a profound change in life that, more often than not, is suffered alone.

So, when we are cut adrift—whether by our own choosing or by the physical limitations of our bodies—it can be disorienting and a lonely journey through a dark sea. We have only to hope to spot a jetty, a strip of coast in the fog where we might attempt a landing. If we're lucky, there might even be a spouse or a dear friend out there, maybe just someone with a light and a welcoming wave who might steer us in around the rocks.

XVIII

How Much Free Will Do You Want?

What CRISPR has wrought

My mom used to give me a hard time because I was a prodigiously bad decision maker as a child. I could be paralyzed by whether to go play soccer or venture down to the creek behind the house. I can still see her shaking her head, a wry smile on her face, "Oh, Adam ..." It was a bit ironic because the basic problem I had I inherited from her. She had an uncanny ability to see the good on both sides of everything.

It got so bad for me that I took a class in high school: Decision Making 101. Yes, it is absurd there was such a class. Had they known, taxpayers would have been outraged. All I remember from it was making long lists of pros and cons for whatever decision we were presented with. Then we got to the decision point where we had to make a leap, this way or that way. And after a semester of making lists, it was no different from before; both leaps looked pretty good to me.

I do remember the rubric of the class though: Decisions were considered good or bad depending only on whether you had enumerated all of the pros and cons at the time of the decision. By contrast, most people in the real world consider decisions good when they get good outcomes, which come long after the decision point. We want prescience, sure things, a fixed table. But the reality is decisions are an exercise in probability. The whole point is that you don't have perfect information about the future.

Even though the stakes get higher, decisions, in a way, get easier as we age. As we become adults, our decisions are no longer made in a vacuum. Most of them are made in reaction to some driving force: circumstances or time. I did this because of that. If I hadn't decided this, that would have happened. Our decisions are free to an extent, but there is usually a condition that frames your choice, steers it, stacks the probabilities, and, in a sense, makes it easier to move one way or the other.

But what if you had more—maybe even absolute—choice? What if your decisions were made in a vacuum, if just about any outcome was possible and certain?

Walter Isaacson has written a very good book on gene editing, a technology dubbed CRISPR, which is a biochemist's convoluted acronym for a complex process bacteria developed over three billion years to fight off viruses. The book, titled "The Code Breaker," centers on Jennifer Doudna and a handful of other scientists who discovered a defense mechanism bacteria evolved to recognize and destroy invading viruses.

We tend to think of viruses—like the COVID-19 virus—as being just our problem, but they have been attacking other life forms, like bacteria, since the beginning.

Bacteria have been evolving for 3.5 billion years. Humans have been evolving for 2.4 million years. To put that in perspective, think about going back in time for all of human evolution—from homo sapiens (us) back to homo habilis, 4-foot versions of us using stones to cut things. Then do that a thousand more times and you get to the point at which bacteria appeared on the planet. That's a lot of time to evolve, and, it seems, they used their time well.

Viruses are much simpler organisms than bacteria; they are little more than packages of genetic material—DNA or its cousin molecule, RNA. Still, they have learned to survive all this time. A virus's sole mission is to inject itself into a living cell—whether bacteria, human, or other animal—hijack the cellular machinery of its target and replicate itself, sometimes killing the host cell in the process.

While scientists debate whether the virus or bacteria came first, safe to say, bacteria have been dealing with invading viruses for billions of years. So, when a virus invades a cell of bacteria, the bacteria takes note. It sends a specific enzyme (called Cas1) to chemically snip out a section of the invading virus's DNA. It then chemically pastes the snippet of the virus's DNA into its own DNA. In effect, it has taken a mugshot of a bad guy. What's more, the bacteria will make a copy of that snippet (called crRNA), which then functions like a "guide," or detective in this analogy, circulating in the cell looking for that particular virus. The next time a virus with that unique DNA signature injects itself into the bacteria, the bacteria recognizes the invader and sends a different enzyme (called Cas9) to chemically eviscerate the virus's DNA, in effect ending the threat. It is a system in which the bacteria can remember a bad guy, then identify and destroy a bad guy—basically what we would call an immune system.

Over the course of about 15 years, Doudna and a colleague, Emmanuelle Charpentier, discovered how all of this works. They won the Nobel Prize in 2020 for their discoveries.

Researchers soon realized that they could also manipulate the "guide" molecule to find whatever stretch of DNA they wanted and cleave it off. They could then insert in its place a stretch of DNA of their choosing. Suddenly, scientists had a cut and paste system—a way to edit genes in bacteria. It wasn't long before other scientists—primarily two fellows named Feng Zhang and Eric Church—figured out you could do the same in a human cell.

What are the implications of that?

The first implication is that a whole host of genetic diseases —cystic fibrosis, for example—could now be edited out of an embryo. The gene that causes this horrific disease would never appear again in the lineage of that embryo. If every family with the cystic fibrosis gene underwent this therapy, the disease would be eliminated from the human genome forever (or, at least, until a random mutation occurred). Short of that, the defective gene in an individual could be edited so that it functioned normally and he or she could live a normal, long life.

Cystic fibrosis is an easy example. But the world of genetic editing quickly gets complicated, as the distinction between treatment and enhancement gets blurry.

The question becomes: To what extent do our faults—say challenges or even disabilities—engender our strengths? I was never big as a kid, so I never played football. I spent all that time playing soccer and became better at that sport. If I were an uncoordinated soccer player, maybe I would have taken up the violin and become a world-class violinist—highly unlikely, but you get the point.

Isaacson, in "The Code Breaker," tells the story reported in the Washington Post of a lesbian couple, both of whom were deaf. They wanted to have a deaf child, so they found a deaf sperm donor and subsequently had a deaf child. Was that morally right? Some say yes, some say no. To extend the example, with the help of CRISPR, a deaf couple could decide to edit out the hearing gene of their embryo, soon-to-be child. Is this inflicting a disability on a child or giving them an experience that the parents feel is valuable to their identities and that of their child?

Yet another complication is that many genes code for more than one trait, and those complexities are not fully understood. Some "bad" genes can confer other unrelated but beneficial traits. Sickle cell anemia is an example Isaacson raises. A person can inherit one gene for it—it requires two to develop this particular disease—and won't get sick. That one gene, though, will give that person an immunity to malaria. That is a benefit; is it a big enough benefit to live with the risk of passing the gene on to a future child who might get a second sickle cell gene from your spouse?

Mental illness provides another conundrum. Though not definitively proven, many mental illnesses are associated with extraordinary creativity. If you knew that causal relationship existed, would you wish it upon your future child? Does society at large want those creative genes in the pool, and does or should society have a say in that?

What about intelligence? To make a sweeping generalization, I bet that most parents would want their kids to be smarter. But how much smarter and in what ways? Some genius kids have a very hard time—socially and culturally—in life. Would you choose that? Should you be able to choose that?

The decisions with CRISPR become almost infinite, and, at this point, they are basically unrestrained by law, convention, or moral guidelines—whether personal or social. This is free will of a different degree and kind. We can only hope that our wisdom has evolved to a degree commensurate with our intelligence.

It makes me think of an unrelated but similar kind of question: If you could choose the day on which you were to die, would you?

I don't think I could, but then again, I never was good at making decisions.

XIX

San Gennaro's Teachings

*Coming to terms
with a handgun*

My first experience with a handgun was not what I expected. I was 17, a freshman in college back East, and my dorm-mate, Mikey, had invited me for fall break to his family's home in Great Neck, New York.

Mikey and I were fast friends: he a quick-witted, feisty Long Islander, me a slower-witted, laid-back Californian. A Butch and Sundance Kid of sorts, curiously thrown together in the fresh-man class of a New England college. Though smart as a whip, Mikey was convinced—or, at least, was able to convince others —that I, like most Californians, spent my days surfing and my nights sleeping on the beach by a bonfire. That piece of cultural fake news notwithstanding, Mikey was, and I'm sure still is, one of the sharpest people I've met. He had the sense of humor and bravado that can take you far in life, particularly in a place like

New York City, which, as it turns out, was just a subway ride away from his home.

Perhaps a generalization, but I have learned that New Yorkers love to impress non city types, beach-sleepers like myself, with their grit and savvy in the urban jungle that is Manhattan. And there is something to be said for that. There are skills and knowledge that can keep you alive in a sometimes-dangerous place. Mikey was no different.

So, one night, Mikey took me to the Feast of San Gennaro, which is held every year on Mulberry Street in the Little Italy section of Manhattan. It is an 11-day event of food bazaars, carnival rides, souvenir hawking, and general revelry, all celebrating San Gennaro, the patron saint of Naples.

Mikey and I had a grand time; we ate, drank, played stupid carnival games, drank some more. When the bars closed, which, remarkably, is at 4 a.m., we started walking in search of a subway stop. There was no Google Maps back then, so finding a subway stop involved memory and intuition. Turns out, we had neither that night.

Before long, we were lost in the Bowery section of the city. The streets were empty save for a sprinkling of drug dealers and homeless people. And there we were, two little white guys— if you stacked both of us head to tail, we could barely dunk a basketball—walking aimlessly through a landscape in which we did not belong.

As if on cue, a group of young men—Hell's Angels I came to learn—seemed to come out of nowhere. They were on the other side of the street walking toward us, eight or nine of them. They were joking among themselves, seemingly oblivious to us. Then, of course, they crossed over to our side of the street.

"If we go now, we can outrun these guys," I said.

"No, no, just be cool," Mikey said. "Keep moving, don't look them in the eye."

This struck me as something you might tell someone confronting a bear, not a pack of menacing psychopaths.

With the moment to flee vaporizing, the Hells Angels blocked our way, then formed a tight circle around us. There was a greeting of some sort, whatever you say to angry bikers. Then there was some jostling back and forth. We were now two play toys in a dog pen. Mikey and I tried to be "cool," but we weren't cool. Then a guy who looked as I imagined Jesus to look pulled a pistol from his leather jacket and pointed it at my forehead. I remember thinking two things: this is a dumb-ass way to die, and my mom is going to be unbelievably pissed off at me, dead or alive.

When Jesus pulled the trigger, nothing seemed to happen— until it did. A squirt-gun load of water splashed across my forehead and dribbled down my face. And then the laughter began—cackling really, hyena-like. We just took it. What else are you going to do? When the laughing finally subsided, we were dismissed.

In the end, I could hardly blame them. They were just a bunch of mates looking for a good laugh on a Friday night. Worse things happen to punks in the wrong part of town.

y second experience with a handgun was a month ago.

In the fall, I like to hunt elk, which usually involves hiking mountain ridges in the pre-dawn hours. It is not unusual to come across bear, mountain lion, or wolf tracks in the snow. It can be a little creepy hiking about in the dark by yourself. After a few such experiences, I had decided I would get a handgun in case I were ever to surprise a predator. The chances that this Sundance Kid could out draw a pouncing mountain lion are slim to none. Still, it would make me feel better. No one wants to get eaten without a fight.

So, the other day, when I was in Boise to fetch my daughter from the airport, I had about 30 minutes to kill before her flight arrived. On a whim, I stepped into a gun shop to look around.

It is no exaggeration to say that it took about seven minutes to purchase my first handgun and the requisite ammunition. I gave the shop clerk my name and address, birthday, then testified in so many words that I hadn't done anything bad recently. There was, ostensibly, some sort of check done on me, but I really wonder how much could have been done in the three minutes it took (the clerk had spent at least four minutes typing things up, ringing in the sale). All in all, browsing included, I was out of that store in 10 minutes, gun and ammo in hand and on the streets of Boise.

It was amazing, and—I admit—convenient as could be. I was on time to pick up my daughter at the airport. But the rub is— and you'll just have to take my word for it—I'm one of the good guys. I've never committed a crime, though I did shoplift a deck of Jack Daniel's playing cards from Macy's when I was in seventh grade. But that was both the beginning and the end of my life of crime.

So, would I care if someone spent more than three minutes checking me out before turning me loose with a 9 mm? Not one bit. Have at it. I have all the confidence in the world that should I choose to buy a gun next year, I'll be able to do just that. And the year after that.

Sadly, a lot of innocent people—most poignantly young children who don't even have a dog in this stupid fight—are being lost to gun violence. A modest effort to regulate the industry seems to me pretty reasonable. The slippery slope argument—that some sensible regulations today will lead to the government taking our guns tomorrow is hogwash. The Second Amendment will be in place until the end of time. The NRA and the Supreme Court will make sure of it. Can't we, at least, learn to live with a little common sense until then? And I mean that literally.

Back to San Gennaro. Did I mention that he, a Bishop, was martyred? In trying to intervene in the religious persecution of some Christians by the Roman Emperor Diocletian (A.D. 284-305), San Gennaro was promptly arrested and sentenced to be fed to the lions in the amphitheater at Pozzuoli. As the miracle goes, the lions refused to eat him and simply knelt before him out of respect. Sadly, San Gennaro was resentenced, and officials promptly lopped off his head.

Sometimes a guy can't win.

XX

Life During a Pandemic

What disease can teach us about ourselves

was lucky; I didn't get a very bad case of COVID-19. Plenty of friends did, however. A common symptom of those and others was what became known as a COVID fog: a general fuzziness, inability to think clearly, or to project thoughts forward.

Disease or no disease, it feels as if we have all been living in a fog for the past 18 months. The gauzy nature of the time, however, comes into stark focus when we contemplate the death involved: 1,030,000 people in the U.S. have died from the disease as of August 12, 2022. The Vietnam War lasted 12 years and claimed 58,220 American lives; the U.S. involvement in World War II lasted almost four years and cost 407,316 lives. What we often think of as the most cataclysmic event of the last century, and one that took two atomic bombs to end, doesn't even come close to the devastation caused by this tiny virus. How tiny? You'd have to line up a thousand of them edge-to-edge to stretch across the diameter of a strand of hair. That's a different kind of atomic bomb.

That being said, we are emerging from the fog. This is what I've learned:

Families are still the touchstones of our lives. Whether by choice or necessity, millions of people rediscovered the joys and challenges of living as a family. College kids moved back in, high schoolers spent giant stretches of time at home, toddlers soaked it all up. I, for one, know I learned things from my kids, laughed with them, watched them mature through a crisis, and otherwise enjoyed every second together that I never would have had absent COVID. That is not a unique experience. Amid the great losses, siblings bonded, parents listened to their kids, talked to each other, and found a way forward together. All of the pre-pandemic discourse about the death of family life proved to be all sound and fury.

Smart people come to the rescue. For the past few years, it has been fashionable to distrust, even disparage, the elite, the educated, the smartest guys in the class. The fact is very smart people saved us from total ruin. Our arsenal of vaccines has proven to be the only tool that will potentially clear us of this mess and save hundreds of thousands, if not millions, of lives. Masks, social distancing, and moving outdoors work for a while, but they are not sustainable over time. People just get tired and give up. While it is not as sexy as a moonshot, what all those scientists and engineers did to create multiple successful vaccines in a year—with some using an entirely new technology, mRNA

—is just as miraculous. Traditionally, vaccines have taken, on average, nearly 10 years to develop. Thirty years in, we still have no vaccine for HIV.

Sometimes the smart people are also the brave people. I am thinking of one friend, an ER doctor—of which there are many, and nurses, too—who went to work in the ER, day after day, when the infection rate was out of control. In helping others, not only was her health at risk, so was that of her husband and children. That is a rare sense of duty and a true belief in equality that many of us would struggle to live by. It is a display of valor that played out in hospitals and clinics across the nation.

Choosing ignorance is a luxury we cannot afford. I have a friend who during the height of the pandemic was driving through a rural area of Idaho and stopped for some gas. He masked up, went into the convenience store at the station and was greeted by a clerk, an elderly woman. "Hey, what's with the mask?" she bellowed.

"I don't know, I'm just doing my thing," my friend replied.

"Don't you know, those masks don't do shit," she said. "That virus can go right through porcelain."

Well, no, it can't. And how hard would it be it be to verify that? Certainly, there are structural and socio-economic reasons for ignorance that are excusable, but when we choose ignorance because it is an easy path, or it nicely fits what some other clown is telling us, then that's when we've lost our way.

What you can't see can kill you (and maybe save you). There was a book I was fascinated by as a kid: "The Microbe Hunters," by Paul De Kruif. It details the pioneers of microbiology, including the Dutch scientist Antonie van Leeuwenhoek who fashioned the first microscope in the 1670s and began looking at life invisible to everyone else around him, and Louis Pasteur in the 19th century who was the first to hypothesize a theory of vaccination and then actually formulate one (for rabies).

Much of the world is starting to appreciate now what these guys understood several hundred years ago: There is a complex universe of life existing at scales we cannot see—bacteria, algae, fungi, protozoa, viruses (debatable as to whether technically "life"), prions, and a few other creatures. Some can harm us; others can help.

But if we've learned anything over 18 months, it is that biological life is increasingly interconnected. There is no longer a distinction between the human world and the natural world, whether macroscopic or microscopic. I live in the West, which is wrapped up with the part-myth-part-fact idea of self-reliance and the "independent" man, or woman. It seems a bit of a canard in a shrinking world. No one is truly independent anymore. We all share air, land and water more intimately than ever before. As our habitats increasingly overlap with the habitats of the natural world, so will these microbes increasingly enter our lives. We've already seen it: HIV, Ebola, avian flu, bubonic plague, COVID-19. I suspect others will emerge.

Hopefully, our means for dealing with them will improve. Maybe a new awareness of the invisible world will help. Maybe we'll continue our now more vigilant personal hygiene practices. Maybe we'll remember the value of hard facts, the scientific method, and independent thinking. Maybe we'll be more aware and caring of the vulnerable. Maybe we'll make a little space for others. Maybe.

Viruses we are not. If there was ever any doubt that we are social creatures, it has been dispelled by this disease. Zoom calls were sort of novel at the beginning—cocktail parties by computer, meetings in pajama pants and button-down shirts. But so much is lost when we are not in the same space, literally. Spontaneity, social cues, humor, body language—all of the things that help us navigate and enjoy life are muted to death in a Zoom call.

What's more, innovation and creativity demand human spark. And commerce depends on relationships, which, in turn, depend on real, physical interactions. I have no doubt our lives will return to pre-pandemic vitality. Our social nature is irrepressible.

In the end, what is a virus? It's a bunch of genetic material, basically proteins. Its sole directive is to reproduce, be alive, if you will.

Humans, too, are a bunch of genetic material trying to live and reproduce. But we want more. Where we differ from our little cohabiters is that we are conscious of life. We know that we are alive. And with that comes a universe of emotion, the true distinguisher. Unlike other creatures further back on the evolutionary path, we want and need to feel the world, feel others in the world, know anguish, heartache, joy, grief, pride, and all the rest of it. Take away that, and we're just a speck in someone else's microscope.

XXI

Balancing Act

A nation tries to find its footing

There was a book published in the 1990s that I never read: "Men Are from Mars, Women Are from Venus." I felt I didn't really need to read it. The gist of the book seemed self-evident from the title. Luckily for the author, John Gray, upwards of 15 million people did read it, or, at least, bought it.

In thinking about the current abortion storm set off by a leaked Supreme Court draft opinion, that title somehow popped into my head. It seems to me that Mr. Gray might have been on to something 30 years ahead of his time. In the abortion debate today, we have two sides squared off in an epic battle fighting over different things using different languages.

One side is talking about morality and homicide, the other about equality and privacy.

The communication schism in the abortion universe, however, doesn't break along gender lines. It would take a social or political scientist to parse that, but I would say the toxic brew we're all stewing in comprises elements of political party, gender, socio-economic status, and rural-urban demographics.

The short of it is we have protesters menacing Supreme Court Justices at their homes and state legislators in places like Louisiana introducing bills that define all abortions—whether in cases of rape or incest or anything else—as homicide.

Where in the world is this going?

In one sense, the abortion conundrum we face was borne of the Reconstruction Era after the Civil War. Southern states began enacting laws that restricted the civil rights of former slaves. To balance that effort, Congress came up with the 14th Amendment, which states had to ratify if they wanted to rejoin the United States. The first section of it follows:

"All persons born or naturalized in the United States and subject to the jurisdiction thereof, are citizens of the United States and of the State wherein they reside. No State shall make or enforce any law which shall abridge the privileges or immunities of citizens of the United States; nor shall any State deprive any person of life, liberty, or property, without due process of law; nor deny to any person within its jurisdiction the equal protection of the laws ... "

When the amendment was ratified in 1868, the intent of it was to prevent the states from infringing on a citizen's rights without going through the court system. In the century and a half since then, Supreme Court has further expanded "due process" to recognize three elements of the concept: procedural protections, "incorporation of rights against the states," and "substantive due process."

The first is what you would expect—right to notice, right to be heard, right to a trial by jury.

"Incorporation of rights against the states" simply means that the Bill of Rights (first Ten Amendments) must be applied not only "against" the federal government but "against" the state governments as well. Basically, states had to recognize the Bill of Rights as state law, too.

Substantive due process refers to the position first adopted by the Supreme Court in the early part of the 20th century that citizens have rights that are not explicitly enumerated in the Constitution but are so "substantive," or important, that they warrant protection. The "right to privacy" was one such right that the Court recognized in 1965 when it held that states could not ban married couples from using contraception (Griswold v. Connecticut).

In 1967, the right to privacy was cited again in protecting the right of interracial couples to marry (Loving v. Virginia). The right of unmarried couples to use contraception followed in 1972 (Eisenstadt v. Baird). Then came Roe in 1973. Same sex marriage (Obergefell v. Hodges) was affirmed in 2015 under the same reasoning.

In the Roe v. Wade case, the Court held that a woman does have a right to have an abortion under the 14th Amendment's due process clause (substantive due process and the right to privacy) but that it wasn't absolute. There would be a timeline (the trimester framework) with which states could regulate abortion. The framework would revolve around "fetal viability," the point at which a fetus could survive outside the womb (with medical assistance). Justice Blackman noted in his opinion that the point of viability was when a fetus "has the capability of meaningful life outside the mother's womb." Medical science has determined that to be at 24 weeks.

Basically, the justices ruled that in the first trimester the state (Texas, in this case) had no say in the matter. In the second trimester and post viability, states could regulate abortions when the health of the pregnant person was involved. In the third trimester, which is beyond the point of fetal viability, states could restrict all abortions save those that were necessary to protect the life of the pregnant person.

Why did the Supreme Court position the right to have an abortion within a time framework?

Texas had argued that life begins at conception, as Catholicism would hold. So, by that line of reasoning, a fetus becomes a "person" with the Constitutional protections that affords. The justices could not find support for that argument in the Constitution, only that those "born or naturalized" (citizenship clause, 14th Amendment) in the U.S. were protected by the Constitution.

They also noted that in contrast to Catholicism, Judaism deemed life to begin at birth, and, further, that doctors, in general, considered life to begin somewhere between conception and birth. So, they tried to find a balance at which point the pregnant person's rights ended and the unborn fetus's began. The balance point was fetal viability.

In 1992, the Court upheld the right to abortion under the 14th Amendment in Planned Parenthood v. Casey but refined the Roe ruling to say that before fetal viability, states could not place restrictions that created "undue burdens" on the pregnant person.

Subsequently, there have been other abortion-related cases, but none more consequential than the current one before the court, Dobbs v. Jackson Women's Health Organization. The case concerns a 2018 Mississippi law (unenforced to date) that bans abortions after 15 weeks of pregnancy. At its heart, the case questions whether the fetal viability framework is a valid means for determining restrictions on abortion.

As most of the world now knows, a leaked draft majority opinion written by Justice Alito appears to short circuit the viability question altogether. It states, in part, "We hold that Roe and Casey must be overruled. The Constitution makes no reference to abortion, and no such right is implicitly protected by any constitutional provision ... We therefore hold that the Constitution does not confer a right to abortion ..."

He goes on to write that the issue should go back to the states and let democracy work its magic, one way or the other.

So, according to this draft—which will likely change but not substantially—there is no right to privacy in the due process clause of the 14th Amendment, nor is there other mention of abortion in the rest of the Constitution. Alito's opinion, if it holds, takes a strict textualist approach that will eliminate the right to privacy, and, by extension, a federal protection of abortion. Consistency of logic would suggest that contraception, same-sex marriage, and inter-racial marriage would also become illegal again.

There have long been textualist and/or originalist justices—those who rely solely on the literal text of the Constitution to make rulings—and those who take a more pragmatic approach and do their best to reconcile a document written 235 years ago with an ever-changing society and slate of issues that didn't exist then.

What do I think? It doesn't really matter to anyone what I think, except perhaps to my wife and daughters. But, for what it's worth:

I think the framers were brilliant, but they weren't prescient. In trying to govern a country in a world far different from that of its origins, we have to use some common sense and judgement to find our way. No laws written in the past or future will ever foresee or anticipate the continuous spectrum of greys with which the world presents its problems. Reconciling our laws with the realities of life is not new, but it is necessary.

I also think government is necessary, albeit frustratingly inefficient. Lincoln put it well: "The legitimate object of government is to do for the people what needs to be done, but which they can not, by individual effort do at all, or do so well, for themselves."

That position notwithstanding, I think that a right to privacy has been a vital foil to government intrusion into private life—whether concerning marital or sexual issues, health information, employment, religion, or reproductive decisions—for almost as long as I have been alive. So, yes, I value it and think it is in keeping with the entire thrust of our Constitution, which seeks to hold a healthy tension between a government and its people. And if there is a right to privacy, then surely what a woman does or doesn't do with her body falls under it.

Nothing is black and white, especially abortion. No rights are absolute. Restrictions—as there are on the First and the Second Amendments, among others—make constitutional rights workable in a free society.

One must define the point at which a mother's rights end and the rights of the potential life of a fetus begin. Clearly religion can't be used to find that point; one could never reconcile the theory of life of Catholicism and Judaism, let alone the dozens, perhaps hundreds of religions out there. Choosing one to establish a restriction is tantamount to establishing a national religion.

I was educated as a scientist and grew up in a medical family, so I put my faith in science to find that point, which happens to be at 24 weeks. That may change as medical science advances; so be it. A fetus with no potential for life outside the womb, with or without medical help, does not equate to life in my view. For others it may, and they should be free to choose not to have abortions.

But liberty—being able to do and say what you want—is fundamentally protected if and only if one's liberties don't impinge on someone else's. A theory of life based on repeatable scientific findings and divorced from all religions—fetal viability—preserves that compact.

Finally, I think Alito's argument that the issue belongs at the state level for democracy to work out is a bit of a cop out and a straw man of sorts. Perhaps he has been in his chambers too long to notice, but we have gerrymandered ourselves into a panoply of red and blue supermajority states. To further exacerbate the division, people have begun fleeing to states where they see birds of a political feather. So, Alito's solution of tagging the states "it" ensures we'll end up with 20 or so states with total abortion bans, criminal charges for physicians, nurses and other accomplices and the balance of states with some legal abortion and varying restrictions. It wouldn't be much fun living in a nation like that. What's more, it doesn't sound much like "... equal protection of the laws," words that definitely are in the Constitution.

If our Constitution is about anything, it is about balance. It is about balancing government and the people, federal government and state government, the three branches of government, majority rule with minority rights, liberty and equality.

Right now, an entire nation of people seems unsteady. But we better find our balance soon. Get too far out of balance and, like the old nursery rhyme says, "Ashes, Ashes, We all fall down."

Post script: The Supreme Court did, in fact, overturn Rove v. Wade and Casey v. Planned Parenthood on June 24, 2022, holding that there is no Constitutional right to abortion. With this decision, the power to regulate abortion is fully in the hands of the states.

XXII

Eulogy for a Gentleman

Tom Royce White

Work together on a mountain for 20 years—as Tom White and I did—and you'll pretty much do anything for each other.

This is not how I expected that promise to play out, but a promise is a promise.

I've never been a fireman, or worked on an ambulance, but I imagine ski patrol life is similar to life in the firehouse. The quarters are close. We pretty much eat all day long. There is always plenty of physical work to go around, and there is time. We spend a lot of time together—hours on end, really. Life in the shack—and in the firehouse, I suspect—comprises long stretches of time punctuated by some intense moments.

Being marooned with a bunch of people like that for years on end is like being part of one big, strange marriage. And like any marriage, one can fall into the little traps of the arrangement: taking each other for granted, getting annoyed by each other's jokes you've heard a hundred times, odd tics and habits that over long stretches of time seem to morph into enormous character flaws.

Tom never fell into those traps. After being up all night at the firehouse, he showed up to work at the mountain upbeat, professional, always pleasant. Tom was a gentleman, in every sense of that word. He was the steady hand in the room who most days had a wry smile on his face.

I loved Tom's humor; it was quiet and quick, never mean-spirited. He was so self-effacing that if you weren't paying attention, you could miss the jabs and witticisms. Things rarely went by Tom, and he pulled his humor from his vest at just the right times.

It is a critical talent to be able to laugh and make others laugh in a line of work that is anything but funny. Humor keeps you in a sort of universal balance when you live your life on call, waiting for something bad to happen to someone else. Like crazy Labradors bred to retrieve, first responders are wired to seek out the sick and the injured. It sounds awful and weird, but the truth is we all want to be where the trouble is the thickest.

Sometimes we get more than we bargain for. More than once I have been on wrecks when I could feel events overtaking me. And then Tom would show up on scene, and I knew we would be okay. He was always calm. He knew what to do, and he did it. He was the guy who could see the problem clearly, simplify the problem, then solve it. Tom was a hero with no ego.

Sam, Will, and Lisa, know this if nothing else: what your father did for a living was honorable—about as honorable as it gets in life. With ski patrolling, firefighting, EMS work—there's not a lot of money, there's less fame, and it's stressful. You can't make mistakes with other people's lives. Tom White spent all of his days and nights, used all of his wits and his wisdom to help those who were in need. I can't imagine anything more noble.

When people leave us, however they leave us, the why of it always haunts us. It can consume us if we are not careful. And this is especially true for first responders because it is our job to fix things. We find people at some of their worst moments in life and try to make it just a little bit better. And we almost always do. In those rare but devastating times when we don't make it better, we are left wondering: What did I miss? What could I have done or said differently? Why didn't I think of this or that? There are a thousand whys.

I have a 3-year-old daughter, and the other day we were out stomping in puddles. At one point I got out ahead of her, then looked back. She was just standing there. I asked her what she was doing. "I had to stop to think, Dad."

It struck me then that there is a remarkable moment in life when an inner world suddenly appears before us. At that point, we don't just live in the world; we can think about the world. We can speculate, fantasize, play out scenarios. We can think anything we want, and it's all ours. It can be the most liberating thing in the world, but it can be terrifying, too.

For better or worse, we all experience the world uniquely, through the filter of our thoughts—both the world's splendor and its anguish. So as close as we get to one another—whether it's our husband or wife, colleague or friend—we don't always see the world the same way. That makes the sorting out of the why of things very difficult.

There is something else to consider.

There are hundreds, probably thousands of people out there who got through a time they probably thought they could not get through but for Tom's help. He was there at the exact right moment, with the exact right skill set and with his compassionate nature. These people he helped were strangers for the most part. People he would never see again.

If you saw five strangers in need every day, would you give them each $10? Would you give them $100? Or maybe an hour of your precious life? What would you give?

Tom freely gave a piece of himself to every patient, every day, every year. That is a profound gift. It's possible he just ran out of himself to give.

I was trained as a scientist, and it was drilled into me that every problem has a solution. While I still think that's true, I've also come to realize that not all things in this life are knowable.

Last, I would like to share a brief story from a long time ago because I think it pertains to our situation here.

As it happens, 26 years ago today, another Sun Valley ski patrolman, Jim Otteson, died. He was caught in an avalanche north of town. I was a young ski patrolman working that day, and through a quirk of circumstance ended up at the scene near Baker Creek. Several of us tried to revive Otto at the scene. We tried all the way back to town, then in the ER.

After the doctor pronounced Otto dead, I walked out to the loading dock of the old Moritz hospital. There I sat on the cold concrete and felt the full weight of the loss come down on me. The guilt, the sense of failure was about as much as I could take; Otto was literally in my hands. And then a friend, the ski patrol director at the time, sat down on the loading dock next to me. We didn't talk. Minutes went by in silence. Then, he simply rested his hand on my shoulder and kept it there. With that one gesture, I felt the guilt and confusion and anger of that day wash away.

This is what a lot of people in this room do—we take care of people. But it doesn't always take the form we expect it to. I couldn't bring Otto back. And we can't bring Tom back. But we can, with a hand on a shoulder, maybe a smile at the right moment, help each other take a step forward into a brighter moment.

I know with all the certainty in the world that Tom White would do that for me.

Tom Royce White: (6/7/1971-1/29/2022)

XXIII

Evangelist

*'The Life You Save May Be Your
Own'*
—Flannery O'Connor

Drive east out of the San Francisco Bay Area toward the Sierras and it's not long before the crush of humanity gives way to the roll of the California earth: golden grasslands peppered with blue oaks. The towns get smaller: Knight's Ferry, Chinese Camp, Big Oak Flat, Casa Loma.

From there, the Lumsden Road—built by the Lumsden brothers in the 1890s to harness water for mining—descends the Tuolumne canyon. The road is all dirt and turns but eventually delivers one to the Tuolumne River. While the river has a tortured history, here it is clear and wild, officially "Wild and Scenic."

Of course, early in the last century it was wilder and more scenic. Then came the 1906 San Francisco earthquake, which, with the associated firestorm, destroyed the city's water system.

Before long, however, the city had purchased water rights to the Tuolumne and, by 1923, despite the strenuous objections of John Muir and the fledgling Sierra Club, had constructed the O'Shaughnessy Dam at the cost of $100 million and the lives of 67 men and one woman. The resulting Hetch Hetchy Reservoir buried a huge chunk of Yosemite National Park. That notwithstanding, the dam and 160 miles of gravity-fed aqueduct now deliver clean water to 2.7 million people in the Bay Area. Eighty-three miles of river remain.

As a commercial whitewater guide in the 1980s, I missed a lot of the historical context. The "T" as we called it, was simply a great place to guide. It was a two- or three-day trip with nonstop class IV whitewater running through a pristine canyon. That's not to say it wasn't intimidating. As guides, we were nervous most of the time—come low or high water.

It began with the 6-mile drive down the precipitous Lumsden road in a truck overloaded with gear and guides. On rainy, muddy drives to put-in, it was always a question as to who got to stand on the back bumper and who had to be in the cab. The thought was that when the truck started sliding off the road and down to oblivion one could, from the back bumper, make some sort of superhuman leap to safety. Fortunately, we never had to test the theory.

Other guides, from other outfitting companies, seemed not to be nervous in the least. Often we arrived at put-in early in the morning to find the crew of a particular competing outfitter rigging their boats. They were stringy, tough looking guys with tattoos, always smoking cigarettes and drinking whiskey. The Rolling Stones blasted from their truck speakers. They seemed as cool as could be.

I worked for an outfitter that went by the name Echo, which, unlike the other outfitters' names, wasn't an acronym and didn't really mean anything. Nonetheless, we ran great trips; the guests generally loved the experience. But the thing with running the Tuolumne was that no matter how great the trip was going, it somehow felt like disaster was always a couple of oar strokes away. The river is technical, fast, and full of decision points. We were all good boatmen and women at that point, but, as we were fond of saying, shit happens.

So, I was a bit uneasy when Dudley and Marian, John and Mildred (not their real names)—all in their late 60s—climbed in my oar boat at put-in one day. I could see immediately that Dudley was a stern fellow, Marian as sweet as my grandmother. I didn't get a bead on John and Mildred, except to know they were older and frailer than I would have liked.

There is no warm-up on the Tuolumne. Within yards of the put-in is Rock Garden, which is exactly that but with a couple thousand cubic feet per second of water streaming through—basically a big sieve. There is a clean line right of center that runs halfway down the rapid, at which point a boatman must make a deft move left to a different channel.

As it turned out with my four sexagenarians, I wasn't so deft and perched the thousand-pound raft on the rock I was planning to miss. Then I was in and out of the boat, pulling on oars, heaving raft tubes back and forth. More than once, standing knee-deep in the river, I faltered on the slick rocks below, nearly slipping downstream and leaving my charges behind. My four guests eyed me stoically.

The next series of rapids went as smoothly as they ever do: Nemesis, Sunderland's Chute, Hackamack, Phil's Folly, Stern. The mood in the boat, however, was a little less than sanguine. Sour might be the word. I knew what Dudley was thinking: *What in the hell are we doing here? This river is bigger and scarier than they said, and this guide is not as big and strong as he should be.*

Dudley was right.

Then there was Evangelist. Drifting above the drop, I stood to see the rapid in its entirety. Below, one of our other guides, Tom Montgomery, was tied up in an eddy on the left waiting for me to come through. As I picked my line, I gave him a nod.

There are a thousand stories about Tom Montgomery. I'm pretty sure all of them are true. He didn't smoke or drink, didn't eat meat, believed in God, was fitter than anyone I've ever known, and was, of course, good looking with sharp blue eyes and a quick smile. One story was that as a rescue kayaker on Chile's Bio-Bio River (before it was dammed), Tom had been slammed into a rock wall in a rapid called Milky Way. Trapped in a crevice underwater with two broken legs, Tom somehow wriggled his way out and swam to safety.

Then there was his stint in the Marines. He and a high school friend had enlisted because they "thought it would be fun." It didn't turn out to be that much fun. Nonetheless, Tom didn't become your average Marine. After numerous physical tests and competitions, he was recognized as the fittest Marine in the entire Marine Corp.: Mr. Physical Fitness. Such distinctions don't go unnoticed in the military; before long a colonel summoned Tom to his office and offered him an appointment to Annapolis. As it happened, Tom didn't want a career in the military, so said thank you, but no, and that he would serve out his enlistment and go home to Missouri.

It was not the answer the colonel wanted to hear. There was shouting; things were thrown. Marines didn't refuse appointments to Annapolis. Those who did were transferred to a station in the Mojave Desert where miscreants were otherwise taught a lesson. And to that end, a particularly sadistic sergeant subjected Tom all day every day to miles of running, pushups, sit-ups, verbal lashings—in 100-degree weather. Tom took it for a while. Then he snapped.

Being a Missouri boy, he knew a thing or two about snakes. When he happened upon a baby rattler in the desert one day, he scooped it up. He then secreted away the sergeant's canteen, put the snake inside, and replaced the canteen in the sergeant's quarters.

The next day the sergeant pulled Tom aside: "Don't screw with me; I won't screw with you." Tom finished his enlistment without incident.

Evangelist is a sweeping right-hand turn with, among other things, a granite boulder at the apex of the turn splitting the river in two. A guy can make either channel, but he's got to choose. The water moves fast there.

Thinking back on it, I know it was just a second of hesitation. Maybe less. How long does it take to form a fleeting thought, ponder two sides of a decision?

As our raft rode up on to the Evangelist rock, the current flooded in, spun us sideways, then folded the 16-foot oar boat back on the rock like so much Saran Wrap. It happened in seconds.

"Where is my wife?" Dudley screamed.

Guides are taught that when shit happens, the first thing to do is count passengers. And to Dudley's point, there were just two of them in the boat now.

A wrapped oar boat in the middle of a rapid is its own kind of chaos. Oars are swinging around, the rapid is loud, guests scream, coolers and food boxes are flooded, gear floats away. As do people. Looking downstream, I could see frail John bobbing along. But Marian?

I scanned the rapid left to right, upstream, downstream. I scrambled over the load, peering over the tubes and around the gnarled boulder we were pinned to. Then I looked down into the water. Six inches below, in the current slamming the raft, I could see the top of Marian's cropped silver hair.

With Dudley gripping the back of my lifejacket, I moved gingerly headfirst into the current. I could feel Marian's shoulders there—slippery and cold—then her armpits. I heaved on her lifejacket. She didn't move. Was she holding on to the raft somehow? It seemed impossible. I pulled on her again. And again. Then again. Over and over. Had it been a minute? Ninety seconds? More? I'm not sure, but I do know that there was a moment when the future compressed into a millisecond of thought, one that still pains me: It's done. I can't move her. She is dying. She will die. This moment will create ruin.

When I looked up from the water, I saw Tom scrambling over the rocks on shore. Across the channel of whitewater, he was trying to tell me something, but I couldn't make it out. What he couldn't tell me I could see. Fierceness. Certitude. Belief. Strength. Whatever else drives a man like that. And here he was offering it up to me. It was like a bolt of lightning showing me a way back to the world.

I went into the water again, this time feeling a spare oar deep underwater. This is what was pinning Marian against the raft and rock. And for the first and only time in 30 years of guiding, I pulled the Buck knife from the sheath on my lifejacket and cut the 10-foot oar loose. Dudley and I pulled Marian from the current. She was cold and pale and alive.

After that trip, I never saw Marian again. Tom Montgomery and I stayed in touch off and on over the years. We ended up living in the same small town, the place he died in 2003, of colon cancer. He was 40.

I don't really know what Marian or Tom thought of what we had been through. Tom and I never talked about it. I wish we had.

What I do know is that we aren't half the people we become without a rare few who happen to wander into our lives at the right time. It might be for a moment or a lifetime. You won't know. You can't predict who is going to change your life, or at what instant. And the rub is, if you're not careful, those moments can pass you by.

XXIV

Last Word

A mother's wisdom

've lived a lot. I've lived in Africa several years, been initiated into the Kikuyu tribe, hitch-hiked from Victoria Falls to Malawi, swum in a lake with hippos, been stranded in the Sudanese desert, married 21 years, raised two fine sons, gone up rivers in East Kalimantan (Borneo), joined the Peace Corps, known witch-doctors and Ministers, Generals and villagers. I'd like to live a little more, but, unfortunately, I am dying of cancer.

The point is not that one should learn to live a little, but rather that one should live to learn a little ... a little compassion, a little understanding, and, eventually, a little humility.

I wish you well,

Paula

Paula Jean Tanous
(December 28, 1933 – December 5, 1996)

Adam Tanous is a writer, editor and ski patrolman living in the Northern Rockies. When he was 10 years old, enjoying childhood in Portola Valley, California, his family suddenly moved to Africa for a stretch. It was an experience that happily colored the rest of his life. He was subsequently educated at Hospital Hill Primary School, Williams College, Stanford University, and the University of Virginia, earning degrees in chemical engineering and fiction writing. In the early part of his career, he worked as a research scientist in the San Francisco Bay Area but ultimately left that world for the mountains of Idaho to run rivers, ski patrol, and write nonfiction. He continues to live and write there with the help of his wife and three children.